STERLING BIOGRAPHIES

# JOHN F. KENNEDY

## Voice of Hope

Marie Hodge

STERLING

New York / London
www.sterlingpublishing.com/kids

This book is dedicated to my cousin, hero firefighter Stephen Siller. On 9/11 he strapped eighty pounds of equipment on his back and raced through the Brooklyn Battery Tunnel toward his death in the Twin Towers.

On a Sunday afternoon at the end of each September, thousands of people run or walk through the same tunnel to honor his memory. They've raised hundreds of thousands of dollars for the Stephen Siller, FDNY, "Let Us Do Good" Children's Foundation.

A true profile in courage, Stephen left us with the legacy of his indomitable spirit.

STERLING and the distinctive Sterling logo are registered trademarks of Sterling Publishing Co., Inc.

Library of Congress Cataloging-in-Publication Data

Hodge, Marie.
  John F. Kennedy : voice of hope / Marie Hodge.
      p. cm. -- (Sterling biographies)
  Includes bibliographical references and index.
      ISBN 978-1-4027-3232-4
1. Kennedy, John F. (John Fitzgerald), 1917-1963--Juvenile literature. 2. Presidents--United States--Biography--Juvenile literature. I. Title.

E842.Z9H63 2007
973.922092--dc22
[B]
                                                                    2006027364
                    4  6  8  10  9  7  5  3

Published by Sterling Publishing Co., Inc.
387 Park Avenue South, New York, NY 10016
Copyright© 2007 by Marie Hodge
Distributed in Canada by Sterling Publishing
c/o Canadian Manda Group, 165 Dufferin Street
Toronto, Ontario, Canada M6K 3H6
Distributed in the United Kingdom by GMC Distribution Services
Castle Place, 166 High Street, Lewes, East Sussex, England BN7 1XU
Distributed in Australia by Capricorn Link (Australia) Pty. Ltd.
P.O. Box 704, Windsor, NSW 2756, Australia

*Printed in China*
*All rights reserved*

Sterling ISBN: 978-1-4027-3232-4 (paperback)

Sterling ISBN: 978-1-4027-4749-6 (hardcover)

Designed by Dopodomani
Image research by Susan Schader

For information about custom editions, special sales, premium and corporate purchases, please contact Sterling Special Sales Department at 800-805-5489 or specialsales@sterlingpublishing.com.

# Contents

# Events in the Life of John F. Kennedy

**May 29, 1917**
John Fitzgerald is the second of nine children born to Rose and Joseph "Joe" Patrick Kennedy. The Kennedy family eventually settles in Bronxville, NY.

**1935**
JFK begins his studies at Harvard University.

**August, 1944**
JFK's older brother, Joe Jr., dies while flying a WWII navy plane full of explosives to the English Channel.

**August 1–2, 1943**
JFK's patrol torpedo boat is sliced in two by a Japanese destroyer, stranding him and his crew for eight days. JFK becomes a war hero when he pulls himself and most of his soldiers through the ordeal.

**January, 1947**
JFK is sworn in as congressman in the 11th Congressional District, which included Boston and some surrounding areas.

**1947**
JFK is diagnosed with Addison's disease.

**1952**
JFK becomes senator from Massachusetts.

**September 12, 1953**
JFK marries Jacqueline Lee Bouvier.

**1957**
*Profiles in Courage,* published in 1956, wins a Pulitzer Prize for biography.

**November 27, 1957**
Daughter Caroline is born.

**November 8, 1960**
JFK wins the presidential election. He is sworn in as the 35th president of the United States on January 20, 1961.

**April 17, 1961**
Bay of Pigs invasion on Cuba, authorized by JFK.

**November 25, 1960**
Son John F. Kennedy, Jr. is born.

**July, 1961**
JFK creates the Peace Corps.

**October 16, 1962**
The Soviet Union begins building nuclear missiles in Cuba, which eventually leads to the Cuban Missile Crisis.

**August 5, 1963**
The United States, United Kingdom, and the Soviet Union sign the Limited Nuclear Test Ban Treaty.

**November 22, 1963**
JFK is shot and is pronounced dead at Parkland Memorial Hospital in Dallas, TX, at 1:00 p.m.

**November 24, 1963**
JFK's suspected assassin, Lee Harvey Oswald, is shot and killed by Jack Ruby.

**November 25, 1963**
JFK is buried in Arlington National Cemetery.

1917

1963

# An Extraordinary Man

*My fellow Americans, ask not what your country can do for you—ask what you can do for your country. My fellow citizens of the world, ask not what America will do for you, but what together we can do for the freedom of man.*

You've probably heard of John Fitzgerald Kennedy, the thirty-fifth president of the United States. You might have learned that he was killed by an assassin as his motorcade traveled through the streets of Dallas, Texas, in 1963.

But did you know that he almost died before he ever entered politics, when his U.S. Navy patrol torpedo boat, the USS *PT-109*, was sunk by a Japanese destroyer in **World War II**? He survived, came home a hero, and after several years in **Congress**, rose to the presidency. He was the youngest man ever elected to that office.

His presidency lasted less than three years, but he made some momentous decisions that changed the world. He established the Peace Corps, an organization that enabled young Americans to volunteer in developing countries around the world. He helped avert a nuclear catastrophe in the Cuban Missile Crisis, and he sounded the call to land a man on the moon. He also helped support the growing **civil rights** movement.

John F. Kennedy was an extraordinary man living in extraordinary times. Decades after his death, Americans still rank him as one of the country's greatest presidents.

President Kennedy and his wife, Jackie, arrive at Love Field Airport, Dallas, on November 22, 1963. President Kennedy was assasinated less than an hour after this photograph was taken.

# "One Brief Shining Moment"

*Don't let it be forgot*

*That once there was a spot*

*For one brief shining moment*

*That was known as Camelot.*

> —*from the Broadway show* Camelot,
> *words by Alan Jay Lerner*

It was November 29, 1963, only one week after the assassination of President John F. Kennedy in Dallas, Texas. For the better part of that week, the nation had been glued to its TV sets. Americans had seen the terrible events of that day being played over and over again: the president being shot as he waved to crowds from his car and then being rushed to the hospital–too badly wounded to recover. Two days later, they had again watched with horror as the man accused of assassinating President Kennedy, Lee Harvey Oswald, had himself been assassinated in front of television cameras.

A stunned crowd listens to news of the assassination outside a New York radio and TV store.

At the funeral, Jackie Kennedy holds her children's hands as they descend the Capitol steps in Washington, D.C. Behind her are the president's brother Bobby and his sister Jean. Kennedy's brother-in-law, the movie actor Peter Lawford, is on the left.

Americans wept as they watched thousands of mourners file past the president's flag-draped coffin in the Capitol Rotunda to pay their last respects. They had been touched by the grace and courage of the president's widow, Jacqueline Lee Bouvier Kennedy. She had stood calm and dry-eyed, her two young children firmly in tow, through the heartbreaking funeral service and the burial. It had been an exhausting, terrible week—especially for Mrs. Kennedy.

Away from the public eye, at the Kennedy family home in Hyannis Port, Massachusetts, Mrs. Kennedy found her grief mixed with questions concerning her husband's place in history. To her, he was a man who had made the world around him not just a better place but a magical one. She remembered stories about the kind of little boy he had been so many years ago—sickly, often bedridden, but inspired by history and dreaming of its heroes.

She thought of all the children who would read about her husband in history books, and she wondered what they would learn about him. She wanted future generations to see that President John F. Kennedy, too, had been a hero.

So she called on a trusted friend and journalist, Theodore H. White, who had written an award-winning book about President Kennedy's 1960 presidential campaign. White had been writing for *Life* magazine, a glossy weekly publication well known to American readers, about the president's assassination and its aftermath. Mrs. Kennedy asked White to come to Hyannis Port late on the night after Thanksgiving. She had something to say to the world, she wanted to say it through *Life* magazine, and she wanted White to be the one to report it.

It was already time to print the special memorial issue of the magazine if it was to hit the newsstands on schedule. But the sense of history in the making was too powerful to ignore. The editors were willing to hold the presses for the magazine—even though overtime costs at the printing plant amounted to $30,000 an hour, a huge sum of money in 1963. So White set out to meet with Mrs. Kennedy, despite the fact that his mother had just had a heart attack. He left his mother in the care of his wife

The Kennedy family enjoys a summer break at their Hyannis Port home. John pets the Irish cocker spaniel, Shannon, and Caroline strokes the Welsh terrier, Charlie.

and his family doctor, who agreed that White's first duty was to comfort the president's widow.

## Memories of Camelot

When White arrived at Hyannis Port, he found Mrs. Kennedy still dry eyed and composed. He listened for a long time to her rambling, pained thoughts, in which she tried to make sense of the events of the past week and place them in a larger scheme of things. She talked about cradling her husband's head in her lap after he was shot, and about the puzzled look on his face. She relived the chaos at the hospital, where she fought her way into the room where her husband was being treated, despite the doctors' efforts to keep her away. She remembered slipping her own wedding band onto her husband's finger as a symbol of undying devotion, then having the ring retrieved and returned to her later by a Secret Service agent.

But one of the most significant memories was a song from a Broadway musical play. She felt that it would capture the spirit of her husband's presidency in the public's imagination. *Camelot* told the story of King Arthur and the magical land of peace and justice he had founded with his Knights of the Round Table. Jackie—as Mrs. Kennedy was known to the world—remembered and recounted:

> *At night before we'd go to sleep . . . Jack [as Jackie called her husband] liked to play some records . . . and the song he loved most came at the very end of this record, the last side of Camelot, sad Camelot: "Don't let it be forgot, that once there was a spot, for one brief shining moment that was known as Camelot." . . .*

Young Jack Kennedy loved stories of King Arthur's Camelot. This mural shows Arthur watching Joseph of Arimathea lead the brave and pure knight Sir Galahad to his seat at the Round Table.

*Jack loved history so . . . history made Jack what he was . . . this lonely, little sick boy . . . so much of the time reading in bed, reading history . . . reading the Knights of the Round Table . . . for Jack history was full of heroes. And if it made him this way, if it made him see the heroes, maybe other little boys will see.*

By 2 a.m., White was able to phone *Life*'s waiting editors and read to them his account of Mrs. Kennedy's message to America. It was really her plea to history, he said later, to be kind to John F. Kennedy.

Mrs. Kennedy need not have worried. Because of her impassioned plea that sorrowful night, the public would forever see the Kennedy administration as a kind of Camelot, "a magic moment in American history," as White once wrote, "when gallant men danced with beautiful women, when great deeds were done, when artists, writers and poets met at the White House, and the barbarians beyond the walls held back."

## The Show That Inspired Kennedy

The musical *Camelot* first appeared on Broadway on December 3, 1960—just days after John F. Kennedy was elected president. It starred Richard Burton as King Arthur; Julie Andrews as his queen, Guenevere; and Robert Goulet as the dashing knight Sir Lancelot.

The show tells the story of King Arthur's quest to establish a kingdom of peace and brotherhood. He gathers together the Knights of the Round Table to perform heroic deeds that will help make the world a more just place. For a time, all is perfect in the kingdom of Camelot,

Julie Andrews as Queen Guenevere and Richard Burton as King Arthur in the hit Broadway musical *Camelot*.

but eventually Queen Guenevere and Sir Lancelot fall in love, which leads to the downfall of Camelot.

At the end of the story, King Arthur is about to enter into battle against Lancelot, and he realizes that the perfect little world he has created is about to end. He sends a boy back home to tell everyone about Camelot and keep the dream alive. It's then that King Arthur sings the words that so inspired President Kennedy: "Don't let it be forgot, that once there was a spot, for one brief shining moment that was known as Camelot."

As Mrs. Kennedy had probably guessed, not all historians would come to view her husband's presidency as a golden age of Camelot. To millions of Americans for decades to come, however, the idea of Camelot came to symbolize the hope and promise of the Kennedy presidency, when America seemed poised to make the world a better place—and become a little better itself in the process.

President Kennedy—who became known around the world as JFK—had been full of youth, optimism, humor, and idealism. He had thought big, dreamed big, and given young people hope in their government. It was true that his administration lasted less than three years, but for many who lived through it, it was "one brief shining moment," and they would never "let it be forgot."

Five days after taking office, a relaxed President Kennedy impresses the American people at a news conference. It was televised live from the State Department.

# CHAPTER 2

# Growing Up in a Shadow

*I think that if the Kennedy children . . . amount to anything, it will be due more to Joe's behavior and his constant example than any other factor.*

On May 29, 1917, in Brookline, Massachusetts, Rose and Joseph "Joe" Patrick Kennedy Sr. had a son. They named him John Fitzgerald Kennedy, after Rose's father, John Francis "Honey Fitz" Fitzgerald, who had been mayor of Boston.

The happy parents had no way of knowing that their son would become not only a politician himself but the president of the United States. Baby Jack, as he came to be known in his family, was too young to care.

Joseph P. Kennedy cradles his eldest son, Joe Jr. (left), and two-year-old Jack (right).

As the years went by, the Kennedys pinned their hopes for a son who would enter politics—and possibly become president—on their firstborn son, Joe Jr., who was two years old when Jack was born.

In many ways, the Kennedys were a close knit and supportive, if competitive, family. The Kennedy clan included nine children all together. Jack was extremely fond of many of his sisters and brothers, but none of them had a deeper effect on Jack's life than his older brother Joe.

Joseph "Joe" Kennedy Sr., his wife, Rose, and their nine children. From the left, Eunice, John F., Rosemary, Jean, Joseph Sr., Edward, Rose, Joseph Jr., Patricia, Robert F., and Kathleen.

Almost from the beginning, young Joe seemed destined for greatness. He had a politician's charm and a leader's natural sense of command. He was an excellent student and an even better athlete. Teachers and coaches raved about him. He was, in short, a hard act to follow.

But Jack did follow him—into some of the same elementary schools, prep school, and eventually to Harvard University. And while Joe was the kind of boy everyone admired, Jack made people scratch their heads in wonder.

First of all, Jack was a sickly boy. When he was three, he almost died from scarlet fever. During his childhood, he suffered from a variety of diseases and conditions: whooping cough, mumps, German measles, chicken pox, infections, repeated bronchitis, and many others. At age fourteen, he weighed only

Rose Kennedy kept index cards on all her children. This is Jack Kennedy's early childhood medical record.

John Fitzgerald Kennedy
Born Brookline Mass. (83 Beals Stret) May 29. 1917
Has had whooping cough - measles - chickenpox
Had scarlet fever. February 20. 1920. Dr. Reardon
At City Hospital Boston - with Dr. Kily.
Took care of ear.
Has had mumps.
german measles 1928
Schick test 1928
Bronchitis occasionally

117 pounds and had such a thin face that the other boys at Choate, his exclusive prep school in Connecticut, called him "Rat Face."

He also suffered from a mysterious blood condition that reappeared during his college years. Despite long odds, Jack eventually recovered, although he continued to struggle with illness for much of his life.

At Choate, Jack Kennedy seemed to spend as much time in the infirmary as he did in the classroom. Letters back and forth between his mother and the headmaster or his wife were filled with concern about how to strengthen Jack against constant illness or injury. His brothers and sisters joked that any mosquito that bit Jack was taking a big chance, since there was so much sickness in his blood.

Young Jack Kennedy wanted to be a policeman when he grew up. His sister Eunice looks impressed.

# Trouble at School

As if a sickly constitution wasn't enough, the future president also had trouble focusing on his studies and couldn't even keep his room neat. He was the kind of boy whom people liked to call "dreamy," with his head in a book about faraway lands and adventure or famous people in history. Those books were his beloved companions through many weeks spent sick in bed.

He had problems passing science and foreign language classes, although he had a much easier time with courses in English and history. He made friends easily, and no one could refuse him when he flashed that famous smile. At home, Jack often came in late for dinner, which was against the family rules, but the cooks in the kitchen always slipped him a reheated meal anyway. Everyone agreed that Jack was a bright and likeable

★ ★ ★ ★ ★ ★ ★ ★ ★ ★ ★ ★ ★ ★ ★ ★

## The Books Jack Loved

As a child, Jack was seldom seen without a book. He particularly enjoyed stories about heroes or adventure. Here are some of the books that Jack loved best in childhood.

*Treasure Island* by Robert Louis Stevenson

*Kidnapped* by Robert Louis Stevenson

*The Jungle Book* by Rudyard Kipling

*Kim* by Rudyard Kipling

*Uncle Tom's Cabin* by Harriet Beecher Stowe

*Peter Pan* by J. M. Barrie

"Sinbad the Sailor," from *The Arabian Nights*

*King Arthur and His Knights of the Round Table* by Sir Thomas Malory

fellow . . . if only he would knuckle down and take hold, the way his older brother Joe had.

Whether it was because he resented always being second best to his older brother, or because he rebelled against so many adults constantly finding fault, Jack was prone to mischief. He loved to play practical jokes and once got into serious trouble at Choate for starting a club that met in his room every night after

Jack Kennedy (right) and his friends "The Muckers," a group of practical jokers who met in Jack's room. Starting the group almost got the future president expelled from Choate prep school.

## Jack's Mother Thanks Choate

"Again, let me thank you for your interest and patience with Jack. He has a very attractive personality—we think—but he is quite different from Joe—for whom we feel you have done so much.

Sincerely yours,
Rose Kennedy"

supper. His best friend from those days, LeMoyne "Lem" Billings, later recalled that most of the club's activities were pretty harmless. But young Kennedy infuriated the headmaster by calling the club "The Muckers," because "muckers" was the headmaster's word for boys who did not obey the rules. This was seen as an act of rebellion, and it helped cement Jack's reputation among the teachers as a bit of a "wise guy."

Jack loved sports and tried to excel in them as Joe had. Coaches applauded Jack's determination and his willingness to put up a good fight. But because of his slight frame and tendency to get sick or easily injured, it was harder for him to provehimself on the field than it had been for Joe. For years, he watched Joe win important trophies, but Jack seldom took home a trophy of his own.

Despite challenges in his studies and in sports, there were those who saw something in Jack that suggested he had a potential for bigger things. Many years later, after Jack's death, Lem Billings remembered how, even as a fifteen-year-old boy, his friend subscribed to the *New York Times* and read it "religiously" every day. Billings believed that the dinner-table conversations at the Kennedy home, in which Joe Sr. discussed the affairs of the day with his family, helped spark Jack's interest in world events.

Still, Jack's childhood was dogged by the shadow of his older brother. Although Joe Sr. and Rose loved and took good care of

Jack, they couldn't help comparing him to the older brother who came across as a superstar. Joe Sr. didn't like any kind of weakness in a man, and he occasionally made unkind comments about Jack's constant sickness.

## Rivals and Friends

The boys were rivals on a personal level, too. One time they had a bicycle race in which they came at each other head-on, with neither one backing off from the collision (and only Jack requiring stitches afterward). Some historians think that Joe bullied Jack, and there are stories to suggest there is some truth to this.

But Jack fought back, and despite their rivalry, he looked up to Joe as much as anyone else did—maybe more. In later years, JFK would write:

> *I have always felt that Joe achieved his greatest success as the oldest brother. Very early in life he acquired a sense of responsibility towards his brothers and sisters . . . I think that if the Kennedy children amount to anything now, or ever amount to anything, it will be due more to Joe's behavior and his constant example than to any other factor.*

Jack and Joe had a complicated relationship, but it was steeped in its own kind of loyalty. The Kennedys prized loyalty to the family, and particularly to firstborn Joe, because he was being groomed for great things. And even though Joe Sr. created a very competitive atmosphere in the family, he also told the two oldest boys that if they stood together, nothing could stop them. On the

## A Choate Housemaster's Report

Report of John F. Kennedy in his house for the fourth quarter:

I'd like to take the responsibility for Jack's constant lack of neatness about his room and person, since he lived with me for two years. But in the matter of neatness, despite a genuine effort on Jack's part, I must confess to failure.

Occasionally we did manage to effect a house cleaning, but it necessitated my "dumping" everything in the room into a pile in the middle of the floor. Jack's room has throughout the year been subject to instant and unannounced inspection—it was the only way to maintain a semblance of neatness, for Jack's room was a club for his friends.

I regard the matter of neatness or lack of it on Jack's part as quite symbolic—aside from the value it has in itself—for he is casual and disorderly in almost all of 0minute, keeps appointments late, has little sense of material value, and can seldom locate his possessions.

Despite all this, Jack has had a thoroughly genuine try at being neat according to his own standards and he had been almost religiously on time throughout the Quarter.

I believe Jack began to sense the fitness of things after his midwinter difficulties, and he has and is trying to be a more socially-minded person.

John J. Maher

Ten-year-old Jack is photographed wearing his Dexter School football uniform.

touch football field at home, Jack and Joe Jr. and the other children might compete fiercely with one another, but in the outside world, the Kennedys were to stick together.

As the years went by, the family became extremely wealthy and powerful, so there was every reason to believe that they could help Joe achieve political prominence someday.

During Jack and Joe's childhood, their father held a succession of powerful jobs. He was a successful stock and real estate investor and became a multimillionaire during the 1920s. Joe Sr. also became a Hollywood producer, and he owned movie studios and theaters. President Franklin D. Roosevelt appointed him the first head of the new **U.S. Securities and Exchange Commission** and eventually **ambassador** to the United Kingdom.

Long before John F. Kennedy entered politics, the family had become famous for its wealth, its power, and its nine adorable children. The stage was set for a standard-bearer—Joe Jr.—to put the Kennedys on the map.

# CHAPTER 3

# The Power of Privilege

*How much better chance has the boy born with a silver spoon in his mouth.*

I f Jack Kennedy's life as the second son of a large and very competitive family was difficult, it also had its privileges. Being a member of a wealthy, powerful family opened doors for Jack that would not have opened quite so easily for others. Jack saw the power of privilege in his school career, and later in politics; he even felt it in his frequent bouts with illness.

When Jack was not quite three years old, he contracted deadly scarlet fever. Hundreds of children in the city of Boston were battling the disease at the time, and there was only enough space in Boston's hospitals to treat

Jack's grandfather, "Honey Fitz" Fitzgerald—seen here holding Rosemary and Kathleen—was elected mayor of Boston in 1906 and 1910.

During the Great Depression after the 1929 stock market crash, people lost their savings and their jobs. Many stood in "breadlines," waiting for free food.

a fraction of them. But Jack's grandfather, "Honey Fitz," was a former mayor of Boston, and he had the contacts to get Jack a bed in the hospital. In addition, Joe Sr. was able to hire one of the nation's foremost specialists in infectious diseases to treat his son. The hospital stay and the specialist probably saved the future president's life.

Little Jack was so sick that he remained in the hospital for two months. During that time, his father went to church to pray for him every day, and he promised God that if Jack was saved, he would donate half of his wealth to charity. When Jack recovered, his father donated $3,700 to an organization that provided dental care to poor children. Jack's father recovered from losing half his money, though; by the time he died in 1969, his fortune was estimated at half a billion dollars.

The fact that Jack and his brothers and sisters enjoyed a wealthy lifestyle was all the more remarkable because they were growing up during the Great Depression. This period of history, which lasted from the stock market crash of 1929 until the early 1940s, wiped out the resources of millions of Americans and left them without jobs and, often, without places to live. Luckily for the Kennedys, Joe Sr. had had the wisdom to get out of the stock market before it crashed, keeping his fortune intact. He was determined to use it to advance his children's place in the world.

## Young JFK on Justice

What did Jack think about being born into privilege? There is some evidence that he grappled with the issue of inequality, because he realized most boys did not have the advantages he had. Here's an excerpt from "Justice," an essay Jack wrote when he was a student at Choate:

> A boy is born in a rich family, brought up in a clean environment with an excellent education and good companions, inherits a fool-proof business from his father, is married and then eventually dies a just and honest man. Take the other extreme. A boy is born in the slums of a poor family, has evil companions, no education; becomes a loafer, as that is all there is to do, turns into a drunken bum, and dies worthless. Was it because of the rich boy's ability that he landed in the lap of luxury, or was it the poor boy's fault that he was born in squalor? . . . How much better chance has the boy born with a silver spoon in his mouth of being good than the boy who from birth is surrounded by rottenness and filth.

The Kennedy compound at Hyannis Port, Massachusetts, where the Kennedy children spent their summers.

While the Kennedys began their life as a family in a Boston suburb, they eventually had three homes, with plenty of maids, chauffeurs, and other servants. In 1927, when Jack was ten, Joe Sr. moved the family to the wealthy New York suburb of Bronxville. He also bought a mansion at Hyannis Port on Cape Cod, not wanting to abandon his family roots in Massachusetts.

Over the years, the public would begin to associate the home at Hyannis Port with the Kennedy clan. Later on, Joe also bought a mansion in Palm Beach, Florida, where the family often gathered to sail and swim. With frequent trips to Europe, they led a wealthy and privileged existence and spent much time with powerful and prominent people, from movie stars to ambassadors to captains of industry.

The Kennedy children attended the best schools. Joe Jr. and Jack were sent to the Riverdale Country Day School in the Bronx during their elementary school years, and then they headed off to exclusive prep schools to prepare for exclusive colleges.

Joe started at Choate in Connecticut; Jack began at Canterbury, also in Connecticut, but illness forced him out at fourteen—after which he, too, attended Choate. Even when he got into school scrapes, Jack knew he could count on his father. According to his mother, when the Kennedy children got into trouble, their father would say, "'Tell me the truth, and then I will help you,' and then he would go to work and try to get them out of whatever difficulty they were in."

## To Princeton, Harvard, and Europe

When the time came to apply for college, Jack wanted to steer a different course from his superstar older brother. Rather than follow Joe Jr. to Harvard, he applied and got into Princeton University, a prestigious school in New Jersey. But illness forced him out before he completed his first year.

When he recovered, he decided to apply to Harvard, but he did not have the kind of grades from his years at Choate that were usually required by the prestigious university. The

### JOHN FITZGERALD KENNEDY

Born May 29, 1917, in Brookline, Massachusetts. Prepared at The Choate School. Home Address: 294 Pondfield Road, Bronxville, New York. Winthrop House. *Crimson* (2–4); Chairman Smoker Committee (1); St. Paul's Catholic Club (1–4). Football (1), Junior Varsity (2); Swimming (1), Squad (2). Golf (1). House Hockey (3, 4); House Swimming (2); House Softball (4). Hasty Pudding-Institute of 1770; Spee Club. Permanent Class Committee. Field of Concentration: Government. Intended Vocation: Law.

John F. Kennedy's entry in the 1940 Harvard yearbook.

## JFK Asks for a Raise

Despite his family's wealth, the future president was not given an unlimited amount of money to spend as a child. Here is the twelve-year-old Jack's famous plea to his father to raise his allowance, complete with misspellings and other errors:

> My recent allowance is 40¢. This I used for areo-planes and other playthings of child hood but now I am a scout and I put away my childish things. Before I would spend 20¢ of my ¢.40 allowance and In fixe [five] minutes I would have empty pockets and nothing to gain and 20¢ to lose. When I am a scout I have to buy canteens, haversacks, blankets, searchlidgs [searchlights] poncho things that will last for years and I can always use it while I can't use a cholcalate marshmellow sunday with vanilla ice cream and so I put in my plea for a raise of thirty cents for me to buy scout things and pay my own way more around. Finis. John Fitzgerald Francis Kennedy.

Jack got the raise.

students at Choate had voted him "most likely to succeed," but the headmaster wrote that although Jack had "superior mental ability," it was "without the deep interest in his studies or the mature viewpoint that demands of him his best effort all the time." However, Jack had other advantages to offset this. With a prominent father who was himself a Harvard alumnus, and an older brother who was highly respected on the Harvard campus, Jack's admission was a given, and despite his lackluster grades in prep school, he got in. Once there, Jack faced a familiar problem: he was two years behind a brother who was considered the most accomplished and popular boy in his class.

Joe Jr. was a varsity football star and prominent in campus politics, whereas Jack was too physically fragile to play varsity sports and had only modest personal success on the swim team. Moreover, Jack had lost a race for a student council seat at Harvard—not exactly the stuff political dreams are made of. Nevertheless, the younger Kennedy son seemed to mature during his last two years at Harvard, applying himself to his studies in government and international affairs.

*Jack faced a familiar problem: he was two years behind a brother who was considered the most accomplished and popular boy in his class.*

Jack may have had help from his family in this growth process. During the summer after his sophomore year at Harvard, his father sent him and his best friend, Lem Billings, on an extended tour of Europe. It was 1937, and Europe was teetering on the brink of World War II. The trip fired up Jack's budding interest in foreign affairs and gave him insight into many of the nations that would eventually be at war with one another. He returned to Harvard a far more focused student.

In December of that year, Jack's father was appointed U.S. ambassador to the United Kingdom and sent to London, and

On a 1937 tour of Europe, Jack visited the royal chateau at Chambord, France. The trip stimulated his interest in world affairs.

Jack's exposure to international affairs was beginning. When it came time to write his honors thesis—a senior project required for graduation at Harvard—Jack had resources that most students could only dream of. His father paid for him to roam Europe and provided access to the power elite in both Europe and Washington. When his thesis, "Appeasement at Munich," was finished, he had plenty of contacts to get it published as a book. Retitled *Why England Slept*, the book was JFK's assessment of why England had failed to prepare itself for the possibility of World War II. It became a best-seller.

Patricia and Eunice Kennedy go door-to-door giving out bumper stickers during their brother's 1952 Senate campaign. His mother, Rose, hosted 35 afternoon teas to help the candidate.

## Strong Family Ties

It wasn't just the wealth and prominence of the Kennedy family that gave JFK a head start in life. Despite the fact that Joe Sr. had taught his children to be competitive with one another, he had also trained them to support one another in their endeavors. From John F. Kennedy's first run for Congress in 1946 to his campaign for the presidency in 1960, he had the hands-on help of his father, who worked behind the scenes; his brothers, who often did the same; and his mother and sisters. For instance, Rose and her daughters came up with a way to woo women voters by holding social teas at which they would speak of Jack's virtues.

Moreover, Jack was extremely close to many of his siblings and derived much comfort from them. Besides his older brother, there was Rosemary, toward whom he felt protective because she was mentally challenged; Kathleen, or "Kick," with whom he had such a close personal relationship that people often thought they were twins; Eunice; Patricia; Robert, known as Bobby, who became a close adviser and confidant to Jack and later on a senator; Jean; and Edward, known as Ted, who ended up serving in the **Senate** for more than four decades. Ted, the last of the Kennedy children, was born in 1932, when Jack was almost fifteen. Jack requested (and received) the honor of being Ted's godfather.

As one observer said, "it was an exciting home . . . full of fun and games and fascinating talk about world affairs and world leaders. It was hard for them to find anything as attractive outside. This is why they were so attached to each other, and so secure."

There is much evidence that JFK himself thought his family had been a great help in his life. He acknowledged on at least one occasion that his father had made everything possible for him. Even during his presidency, JFK continued to rely on his father for support. His mother later remembered that during an international crisis that ended badly, her husband was "on the phone with [Jack] most of the day . . . At [the] end I asked him how he was feeling and he said 'Dying'—the result of trying to bring up Jack's morale."

The road to the presidency had been paved for a Kennedy son from the time the first child arrived. When the moment came, John F. Kennedy merely followed the markings.

The Kennedy family at home together. Joseph Sr. (seated, left) taught his children to support one another, and they did.

# CHAPTER 4

# War Changes Everything

*11 ALIVE NEED SMALL BOAT KENNEDY*

In World War II, John F. Kennedy held the rank of
lieutenant, junior grade (later full lieutenant), and served
as the skipper of a patrol torpedo boat, or PT for short. On
the night of August 1, 1943, the boat was in the South
Pacific, patrolling waters near the Solomon Islands. On
and around those islands, thousands of Americans had
already died fighting the Japanese. Hampered by severe
medical problems—including ongoing back problems and
stomach disorders—Kennedy had had to use his father's
influence just to get admitted into the navy, and then he
had to use his grandfather's influence to get into the thick
of the fighting.

John F. Kennedy's U.S. Navy identification card.

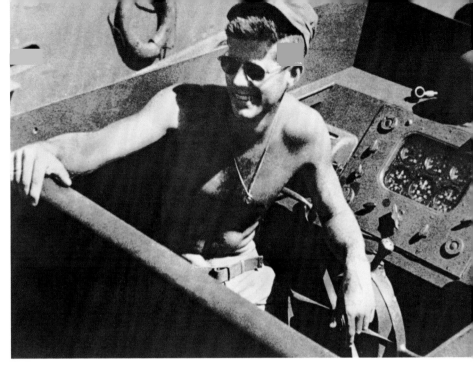

Lieutenant J.G. John F. Kennedy at the controls of *PT-109* in the South Pacific.

On that particular night, fifteen U.S. Navy PT boats gathered in Blackett Strait to stop the progress of a convoy of Japanese ships. But the PT boats were disorganized and communications were bad. Only half the boats fired torpedoes at the convoy, and the attack was unsuccessful.

To make matters worse, eleven of the PT boats had no radar, and the night was extremely dark. Kennedy was in one of the "blind" PT boats with no radar. By the time the Japanese destroyer *Amagiri* was near enough to be seen by the crewmen aboard *PT-109*, it was too late for Lieutenant Kennedy and his crew to evade it. At around two o'clock on the morning of August 2, the destroyer rammed into Kennedy's boat and sliced it in half. He was hurled into the cockpit, slamming his vulnerable back.

Later, Kennedy remembered thinking, "So this is how it feels to be killed." But history was not yet finished with John F. Kennedy—not by a long shot.

The collision threw the entire crew into the water. When *PT-109* began to sink, Kennedy clung to its hull, calling out the names of the men who had been serving under him in order to check whether they were still alive. Two had disappeared, never to be seen again, but ten others had survived, and their skipper was determined that they would live.

*For hours, the eleven men clung to the floating wreck, hoping for rescue. But unbeknownst to them, the other PT boats had decided that there were no survivors, so no one came.*

For hours, the eleven men clung to the floating wreck, hoping for rescue. But unbeknownst to them, the other PT boats had decided that there were no survivors, so no one came. After nine hours, Lieutenant Kennedy started swimming and led the men to a tiny, deserted island three miles in the distance. They named it "Bird Island," because there were so many birds there.

One of the men, Patrick "Pappy" McMahon, was so severely burned that he could not swim on his own. But Kennedy would not leave him. For five hours, Lieutenant Kennedy swam, clenching the ties of the wounded man's life jacket firmly in his teeth and pulling him along. It was an exhausting ordeal and a great act of courage, but Kennedy wasn't through yet.

Taking little time for rest, he left his crew on Bird Island and swam another hour to a passage that the PT boats frequently traveled through. He hoped to flag down one of the PTs and get his men rescued. But once again, fate did not cooperate; the PTs had switched to a different route. When Lieutenant Kennedy realized that he wasn't going to find help this way, he formulated a new plan.

On the morning of August 4, more than two days after the collision, the entire party swam to a larger island named Olasana. Unfortunately, it, too, lacked the drinking water and food they needed to survive. Leaving the men on Olasana, Kennedy and another officer swam to Nauru Island, where they found food and water and a canoe to bring the staples back to the men.

By that time, native islanders had discovered the survivors on Olasana and were ministering to their needs. Kennedy knew that the natives were their best hope for being rescued. With his jackknife, he scratched the following message on a coconut: "NAURA ISL NATIVE KNOWS POSIT [POSITION] HE CAN PILOT 11 ALIVE NEED SMALL BOAT KENNEDY." The natives took the message to Allied

John F. Kennedy (far right, circled) and the crew of *PT-109*. Duty on the 80-foot-long plywood torpedo boat was tough and dangerous.

troops and within two days, all the survivors were rescued by a PT. It had taken eight days, but Lieutenant John F. Kennedy and his men had triumphed over death.

## John F. Kennedy, War Hero

World War II was filled with many stories of heroes, but few became famous. John F. Kennedy once again benefited from being the son of a prominent man. Newspaper stories proclaimed that "Kennedy's son" had behaved heroically in the South Pacific. The story of Kennedy's courage was told and retold in the newspapers and in a famous magazine article. After he became president, the tale was turned into a best-selling book, followed by a movie.

Kennedy received the Navy and Marine Corps Medal and the Purple Heart, a medal of high honor awarded to those who are killed or wounded in service of their country. Long before he was elected president, John F. Kennedy was something of a celebrity to the American public.

JFK kept the coconut shell with its scratched rescue message on his desk at the White House.

## Letter to My Brother the Hero

As part of their friendly rivalry, Joe Jr. was not above ribbing his brother for his celebrity in the wake of *PT-109*. After reading a story in the *New Yorker* magazine about Jack's heroism, Joe sent him a letter with this reaction:

> I read the piece in the New Yorker, and thought it was excellent. The whole squadron got to read it, and were much impressed by your intestinal fortitude. What I really want to know, is where . . . were you when the destroyer hove into sight, and exactly what were your moves, and where. . . was your radar. . . . My congrats on the Medal. To get anything out of the Navy is deserving of a campaign medal in itself. It looks like I shall return home with the European campaign medal if I'm lucky.
>
> ### Your devoted brother Joe

JFK was awarded the Navy and Marine Corps Medal (left) for his courageous rescue of the *PT-109* crew, as well as the Purple Heart Medal (right) for the injuries he endured during the rescue.

## Fate Thwarts the Kennedys

Jack, not Joe, was destined to survive World War II, but at the beginning of Jack's service he jokingly suggested that his death in the war would help support Joe's eventual political career. Here's how their mother put it in a letter to her children:

> Jack, you know, is a Lieutenant, J.G. [junior grade] and of course he is delighted. His whole attitude about the war has changed and he is quite ready to die for the U.S.A. in order to keep the Japanese and the Germans from becoming the dominant people on their respective continents, believing that sooner or later they would encroach upon ours. He also thinks it would be good for Joe's political career if he died for the grand old flag, although I don't believe he feels that is absolutely necessary.

Hyannisport, Mass.
October 9, 1942

Dear Children:

I have been home all the week and it has been lovely here. I have been working in my own little way, trying to get all your clothes sorted out, etc. Dad came home from New York on Wednesday as it was our twenty-eighth anniversary.

We expected darling Teddy home over this weekend, but it seems the little angel got into a water fight in the lavatory and "after he knew his way around he got full of biscuits" and got himself into a little trouble, so he was put on bounds for two weeks. It seems quite unfair because I am sure the boys who were there before provoked him to mischief. Also, these are our last two weekends when he might come home as we now expect to close the house about the 19th. I suppose he has learned his lesson, but a little too late.

June 12, 1944–Lieutenant John F. Kennedy is awarded the Navy and Marine Corps Medal for his heroism.

Did JFK consider himself a hero? Judging by all the available evidence, it seems he took the hoopla (and himself) with a grain of salt. Years later, when he had made it to the White House, a little boy asked him, "Mr. President, how did you become a war hero?"

"It was involuntary," the president replied. "They sank my boat."

In fact, some have suggested that Kennedy felt humiliated by the sinking of his PT. He couldn't wait to get back into battle and prove himself a capable commander.

The rest of the Kennedys had no trouble identifying their Jack as a hero. Joe Sr. remembered how much trouble Jack had gotten into at Choate, and how bleak his future had sometimes seemed. It was clear to him that Jack had grown up and matured into a person of high character.

In a letter to the headmaster at Choate only weeks after *PT-109* hit the news, Joe Sr. wrote: "I can remember the problem child he was at Choate, and it just goes to prove that just so long as a boy is basically right, no matter how many pranks he is identified with, he'll deliver, and that's what Jack did." You can almost hear the buttons bursting off Joe Sr.'s swelling chest, as he delivered this pronouncement.

Through courage and perseverance, Lieutenant John F. Kennedy had survived a terrible ordeal. But the war was not to be so kind to some other members of his family.

## Tragedy Strikes the Kennedys

Joe Jr., a U.S. Navy Air Corps pilot fighting in Europe, found himself living in his brother Jack's shadow. It was an unfamiliar place for him to be. In August 1944, a year after Jack's exploits

*In fact, some have suggested that Kennedy felt humiliated by the sinking of his PT. He couldn't wait to get back into battle and prove himself a capable commander.*

made him famous, Joe volunteered for a dangerous mission, despite the fact that he was scheduled to go home. He and several others were to pilot a plane carrying more than twenty-one thousand pounds of explosives to the English Channel, where they would bail out and leave the plane on autopilot to drop the explosives on the German troops fighting on the coast of Normandy, in France.

Joe's plane never made it. For reasons that never became known, the plane exploded in midair, killing all on board. After his death, he was awarded the Navy Cross, the navy's highest decoration, and a destroyer, the USS *Joseph P. Kennedy Jr.*, was named after him. The man on whom an entire family had pinned its hopes for years had died a hero—but he left his family's dreams in tatters.

The tragedy didn't end there. A short time later, Jack's beloved sister Kathleen lost her husband, a British officer who was the son of the Duke of Devonshire, to a German sniper. And in 1948, three years after the war ended, Kathleen herself was killed in a plane crash. The violent

JFK's older brother, Joe Jr., volunteered as a navy flier and flew dangerous missions over Europe in World War II.

Following Joe Jr.'s death in action, the grieving Kennedy family receive his Navy Cross, the highest honor below the Congressional Medal of Honor.

deaths that began occurring during World War II and its aftermath would eventually become known as "the Kennedy Curse," and other Kennedy siblings, including Jack, were destined to die prematurely as well.

But Jack knew nothing about a curse when he first heard of Joe's death. The younger Kennedy was lying in a hospital bed, recovering from an operation on his back, and the news was the most devastating blow he'd ever been dealt. After Joe's death, Jack put together a memorial booklet with stories and memories from those who had known Joe best, including himself. Among other things, he wrote: "I do not know anyone with whom I would rather have spent an evening or played golf or, in fact, done anything. He had a keen wit and saw the humorous side of people and situations quicker than anyone I have ever known."

The big brother who had been both Jack's deepest rival and his greatest hero was gone. It wasn't difficult for Jack to figure out that his family would turn to him to fill Joe's shoes—but for JFK there was some question about whether that was a role he wanted for himself.

Kathleen "Kick" Kennedy wears the uniform of the American Red Cross in England, where she met and married William Cavendish, Marquess of Hartington. He was killed in action in World War II.

# CHAPTER 5

# Embracing Destiny

*One politician was enough in the family, and my brother Joe was obviously going to be that politician.*

In his play *Twelfth Night*, William Shakespeare wrote: "Some are born great, some achieve greatness, and some have greatness thrust upon 'em." No one will ever know for sure whether John F. Kennedy would have entered politics if his older brother had lived, much less whether he would have made it to the presidency. In a sense, JFK had greatness thrust upon him by an accident of birth and the circumstances of his family's loss.

As JFK once said, "I never thought at school or college that I would ever run for office myself. One politician was enough in the family, and my brother Joe was obviously going to be that politician." For a year or so after Joe's death, Jack wavered. He continued on a path that suggested he might become a journalist or a businessman, or perhaps enter law school. Not long after World War II ended in 1945, his father got him a job with a Chicago newspaper, covering the San Francisco conference that led to the establishment of the United Nations.

JFK (seated, right) received backing in his political career from his father (standing, center) and his grandfather, "Honey Fitz" Fitzgerald (seated, left).

Later, he was sent to Europe to report on other international news.

But Joe Sr. had his heart set on being the father of a president some day. With his eldest son gone, Jack was the next logical choice—even though Joe found him "rather shy, withdrawn and quiet. His mother and I couldn't picture him as a politician. We were sure he'd be a teacher or a writer." Jack's former headmaster at Choate wrote to Rose Kennedy, "I am certain [Jack] never forgets he must live Joe's life as well as his own." Eventually Jack made the decision to enter public life. He compared his father's insistence on that course to the drafting of a soldier. But was pleasing his father the only reason why John F. Kennedy embarked on a political career?

*He loved to ask questions and talk to many different people in order to learn all sides of an issue.*

Life's most important decisions are seldom made on the basis of only one factor. Since the days JFK had first become interested in Europe, before World War II started, he had shown a curiosity about and a passion for foreign affairs. The terrible losses of that war had convinced him that the decisions made by people in power mattered a great deal. He loved to ask questions and talk to many different people in order to learn all sides of an issue. These are traits that serve a journalist well, but there are reasons to believe that John F. Kennedy might not have been content with being a journalist forever, even if his brother had lived.

"A reporter is *reporting* what happened," JFK once said. "He is not *making* it happen. . . . It isn't participating." In the end, Kennedy was so passionate about the world he lived in that he felt the need to wade in and participate, to help create the conditions that would lead to a better world—peaceful, just, and prosperous. He began to think that the best way to participate was to involve himself in public service.

## The United Nations

The United Nations (UN) was created after World War II. Its original aim was to prevent all future wars by guaranteeing every country's security.

The United Nations Headquarters building is in New York City, but the organization came into being in San Francisco in 1945. As a young reporter, John F. Kennedy attended the San Francisco conference at which fifty founding members drew up the United Nations Charter. The fifty—plus Poland—signed the Charter of the United Nations on June 26, 1945. The charter was approved, and the United Nations officially came into existence on October 24, 1945. Under the charter, members agree to settle disputes peacefully.

There are now over 190 member nations, and the UN operates around the world.

## John F. Kennedy Enters Politics

When John F. Kennedy agreed to run for a seat in the 11th **Congressional District** (which included the North End of Boston, East Boston, Cambridge, and two other Massachusetts towns) in 1946, he was in a familiar position—a late bloomer who didn't seem equipped for the task. Just as he had spent years maturing into his schoolwork, he took some time to grow into the role of a candidate. No one who heard him at that early stage of his political career could have ever guessed that one day he would be celebrated as a warm, witty speaker with a magnetic political presence. In the early days, people complained that he spoke too fast and seemed too wooden.

Once again, the young politician had help from his family.

His father financed most of the campaign, leaving Jack free to worry about his speeches rather than trying to raise money. Joe Sr. also helped him overcome his weaknesses. And it was at this point that his sisters and mother began the task of entertaining thousands of women, a few dozen at a time, to expose them to the candidate and his family. The entire family rallied around Jack, intent on beginning the rise to power that had formed so much of their sense of purpose all those years.

Jack worked hard as well, bounding up and down the steps of townhouses to introduce himself to the voters and ask for their support, making appearances at his sisters' teas, and delivering speeches at churches and meetings of veterans' groups.

A small hall is packed for an appearance by congressional candidate John F. Kennedy.

In a way, John F. Kennedy was a strange match for the voters in the 11th Congressional District. Whereas he had been born rich, they were mostly poor or middle class. But, like the Kennedys, many of them were veterans or relatives of those who had died in the war, and they were mesmerized by Lieutenant Kennedy's *PT-109* heroism; it made him seem less like the pampered son of privilege and more like a "regular guy." Kennedy was smart enough to talk about the need for more housing and jobs for veterans, crucial issues for many of the voters in his district. These voters, immigrants or descendants of immigrants themselves, were proud of how far this grandson of immigrants had come.

*For the rest of his life, he never lost a single election.*

All the effort paid off. John F. Kennedy, a Democrat, won the Democratic **primary** handily, which all but assured his election in November, since voters in his district were overwhelmingly Democratic. Much to his family's delight, he was sworn in as the congressman from the 11th Congressional District in January 1947. For the rest of his life, he never lost a single election.

## Living with Pain

As with so many triumphs in his life, Kennedy's electoral success came at a price. For years he had been battling a host of medical ills, including stomachaches, weight loss, and his famously bad back. His brother Bobby once noted that "at least one half the days he spent on this earth," Jack was in pain. The intense pressure of the congressional campaign had made a bad situation even worse. He consulted with some of the best medical experts, hoping to figure out what was wrong with him and to find a cure.

In 1947, his first year in Congress, a London doctor finally identified the condition that had plagued Jack for so long. He had Addison's disease, caused by a hormone deficiency. Treatment with cortisone, a type of steroid, helped some of his symptoms but left his back in much worse shape. Eventually Jack required operations—which were only partly successful. Nevertheless, he continued to press on with his political career.

As a junior member of a legislative body that contained 435 representatives, Congressman Kennedy had little say in much of what went on in Congress, particularly since the Republicans were in control. As he had at Choate, Kennedy chafed under many of the long-established rules and traditions. He hated the fact that as a junior congressman he had little influence on legislation and had to, as Lem Billings put it, "jump a thousand hurdles" to accomplish anything at all. Kennedy served three two-year terms but never had a chance to introduce bills relating to anything he considered important. However, his father helped

JFK beat eight other candidates to become the Democratic congressional candidate. He celebrates victory with his parents and grandparents.

him get a placement on the House Education and Labor Committee, where he was in the thick of battles over federal aid to schools and organized labor.

## Running for the Senate

Almost from the beginning, Representative Kennedy had his eye on a larger prize. Although he spent six years in the **House of Representatives**, he once joked that he "began running for the Senate four and a half years ahead of time." Kennedy called attention to himself by tackling issues that the public—including his constituents—were very concerned about, especially the threat of communism. It was the beginning of the **Cold War**, a period that would last decades, when many in the United States feared that the communist nation of the **Soviet Union** was intent on destroying or infiltrating America and other nations. Kennedy took a strong public stance against the spread of **communism** and was a staunch believer in a strong military to help defend America.

In 1952, John F. Kennedy threw his hat in the ring for the Senate race in Massachusetts. Ironically, his Republican opponent, incumbent senator Henry Cabot Lodge Jr., was the grandson of a man who had defeated Kennedy's grandfather Honey Fitz for the same Senate seat way back in 1916. So in some ways it was a grudge match

Congressman Kennedy tours the Boston waterfront.

# The Two-Party System

America's political system is often described as a two-party system. While there are many political parties in America, two parties win the majority of the votes in most elections—the Republican Party, or GOP (for "Grand Old Party"), and the Democratic Party. This is why Jack and his family were Democrats.

In JFK's time, the Democratic Party was seen as the party of the working class, the people who struggled to make a living and pay taxes, and who perhaps belonged to a labor union. Typically, Democrats were interested in programs such as health insurance, Social Security, and unemployment benefits. People living in cities felt more comfortable in the Democratic Party, where progressive social policies were viewed favorably. In time, the party reached out to African-American voters by taking the lead on civil rights issues. Some Democrats, like JFK, insisted on a strong national defense, especially against the threat of communism.

The Republican Party, on the other hand, was seen as the party of business. Republicans were interested in lowering taxes for businessmen, because they believed that businesses were better than the government at solving problems. Although Republicans had once supported a strong federal government, they now wanted its power decreased in order to avoid its intrusion in business affairs and individual lives. Republicans, too, insisted on a strong national defense against communism.

The donkey (left) and the elephant, (right) symbols of the Democratic and Republican political parties respectively.

for the Kennedys. As always, Joe financed the campaign, and JFK's twenty-seven-year-old brother Bobby became campaign manager. Bobby was a superior organizer blessed with almost unlimited funds, thanks to his father, and he set up a highly effective web of offices and volunteers throughout Massachusetts.

The communist symbol, the hammer and sickle. The hammer represents industrial workers, the sickle symbolizes the peasants.

Nevertheless, Kennedy was not a shoo-in. Lodge, too, was from a prominent family with long ties to Massachusetts politics, and he had the endorsement of the wildly popular Republican presidential candidate, former general Dwight D. Eisenhower, who had been supreme commander of the Allied forces in World War II. At first, election-night results seemed to suggest that JFK had lost. But by morning, he had become only the third Democratic senator in the state's history. Ultimately, what seemed to make the difference was that the voters found Kennedy's personality more likable. He was smart and had been educated at the best schools, yet he acted in a way that the average person could relate to.

John F. Kennedy was thirty-five years old, the age at which a U.S. citizen becomes eligible for the presidency.

# The Senate Stepping-Stone

*I am not the Catholic candidate. . . .*
*I am the Democratic Party's candidate . . .*
*who happens also to be a Catholic."*

W hen Massachusetts voters elected JFK senator, they
gave him a much bigger platform to attract national
attention. Whereas he had been one of 435 members of
the House of Representatives when he was first elected, he
was now one of only ninety-six senators, two from each of
the forty-eight states that formed the United States in
1952. (Now there are fifty states and one hundred
senators.) Furthermore, as a senator, he would have a
much greater chance to affect foreign policy, which had
fascinated him for years. Senator Kennedy set about taking
advantage of the many opportunities that the Senate
provided.

During Kennedy's first year as a senator, he began
working on an economic program that would benefit all of
New England, not just his home state. And in 1954 he
showed he was able to rise above the narrow concerns of
his own region by backing the creation of the St. Lawrence
Seaway. Voters in Kennedy's state feared that the proposed
sea passage between the Great Lakes and Canada would
take business away from the port of Boston. But JFK didn't
think so, and he wanted to prove that he was interested in
the welfare of the entire country. He stood up for what he

## The St. Lawrence Seaway

JFK supported the creation of the St. Lawrence Seaway. The seaway runs from Montreal in Canada to the Great Lakes. Ten villages in the Canadian province of Ontario were deliberately submerged during construction, and six thousand five hundred people had to move to new towns.

The waterway opened in 1959, allowing large commercial ships to navigate from the Atlantic Ocean to the Great Lakes. It takes a typical ship over a week to travel between the Atlantic Ocean and Lake Superior.

believed in despite the risk of angering the very people who had sent him to the Senate.

The young senator also spoke out against President Eisenhower's approach to defense spending. During the Cold War era, many Americans feared that the Soviets were building up a huge military machine. Kennedy thought the president was more interested in weapons for a nuclear war than in troops and equipment for a more conventional or limited war. He considered it a mistake to concentrate all of America's defense systems into one plan of attack. His stance once again placed him on the national stage, and Americans were becoming familiar with his voice.

## Jackie

By 1954, when JFK married Jacqueline Lee Bouvier at St. Mary's Roman Catholic Church in Newport, Rhode Island, he was so famous that three thousand people thronged the streets to catch a glimpse of the wedding party. Jackie, as his new bride was known, was a beautiful young woman from a prominent social set. The couple had met at a dinner party two and a half years before and had had what Jackie later called a "spasmodic" courtship—on again, off again.

Those who knew Kennedy best couldn't help but notice that Jackie was different from the other young women whom he had dated as Washington's most eligible bachelor. She was intelligent and cultured, and she had attended prestigious schools like Vassar and George Washington University in the United States and the Sorbonne in Paris. A friend once observed that when Jackie was in a room, JFK's eyes would follow her everywhere— he found everything she did interesting. Together they were to be a golden couple that was to reign during the White House's Camelot years.

Dwight D. Eisenhower commanded Allied forces in World War II. He was elected president in 1952 and 1956.

# Profile in Courage?

During Kennedy's recuperation from his back operations in 1954 and 1955, he began working on a book that was to earn him even more fame. *Profiles in Courage* was the story of eight United States senators who, at different times in America's history, had risked their political careers to take a stand for what they thought was right.

The issue was important for Kennedy. Although several times he had taken an unpopular position, he also carried the scars of an important battle he had not had the courage to wage, over Republican senator Joseph McCarthy of Wisconsin. By 1954, Senator McCarthy had become one of the most controversial men in America as a result of his warnings about communist infiltration of the U.S. government. That year, he launched a congressional hearing to look into subversion in the army. Because the hearing was televised, the whole country was able to see McCarthy accuse many prominent people, without real evidence, of conspiring with communists.

His fellow senators voted to censure, or condemn, McCarthy for his actions. Every Democrat voted for the censure—except Senator Kennedy, who withheld his vote. Later he said it was because his brother Bobby had been on McCarthy's staff. Whether or not that was so, Kennedy had to defend his actions many times in the years to come.

Senator Kennedy began work on his book *Profiles in Courage* in 1954. It won the Pulitzer Prize for biography in 1957.

*Profiles in Courage* was published in 1956. It became a bestseller, and it received the prestigious Pulitzer Prize for biography in 1957.

JFK and his bride, Jackie, cut their five-tier wedding cake. They became engaged after Jackie returned from London, where she was covering the coronation of Queen Elizabeth II for the Washington *Times-Herald*.

But Kennedy was not there yet. In the year after he married Jackie, his back pain became so severe that he was using crutches to take the pressure off his back whenever he was out of the public eye. He consented to a very risky back operation. The surgery was complicated by his many other health problems, especially Addison's disease. Doctors told him there was a fifty-fifty chance that he would die as a result of the treatment, but they warned him that without the operation, he eventually might not be able to walk at all. According to Rose, JFK told his father that he would rather die than spend the rest of his life "hobbling on crutches and paralyzed by pain."

A raging infection after the surgery put Kennedy in a coma. His family called a priest to give him the last rites, a Catholic sacrament that at that time was given to those on the brink of death. Joe sobbed at the thought that he could lose another son in whom so many of his hopes and dreams had rested. Luckily, Jack pulled through. But the recovery period was long, and the surgery caused more problems, which required a second operation in 1955.

# The 1956 Presidential Campaign

Not long after, in 1956, Kennedy was asked to give a speech nominating the presidential candidate, Adlai Stevenson, at the Democratic National Convention. The convention was televised, and the boyish, appealing young senator made a strong impression on all who saw and heard him. Some people wanted him to run on Stevenson's ticket as vice president—and at one point Kennedy was only thirty-eight votes away from winning enough delegates to secure that spot on the ticket. But many worried that a Catholic vice-presidential candidate would keep many Americans from voting for Stevenson. In the end, the nomination went to Senator Estes Kefauver of Tennessee.

Later on, JFK came to see this as a good thing, since President Eisenhower and Vice President Richard Nixon defeated Stevenson and Kefauver handily in the election. Had Kennedy been on the ticket, many would have said it proved that a

Catholic could not be elected to a high national office, and it might have prevented him from running for president. Kennedy could not help noting that his inability to land the vice-presidential nomination set him apart from his brother Joe and,

Kennedy lies on a hospital gurney after spinal surgery. He suffered from chronic back pain and underwent a number of operations in attempts to find a cure.

JFK with Adlai Stevenson during the 1960 presidential campaign. Stevenson was the defeated Democratic candidate in the 1956 presidential election.

in the end, made him a more likely candidate for president. In the same circumstances, "Joe would have won the nomination," JFK once said. "And then he and Stevenson would have been beaten by Eisenhower, and today Joe's political career would have been in shambles."

By 1959, Kennedy had been in the Senate for six years and was ready to make his move for the presidency. As a member of the Senate Foreign Relations Committee, he had learned to speak with authority on foreign affairs. As a member of a subcommittee investigating unions, he had fought against criminal activity in labor unions and once again earned a place in the national spotlight for his courage. He had crisscrossed the nation on behalf of Stevenson and Kefauver, shaking hands and letting voters get to know his face.

# Problems on the Presidential Trail

Kennedy encountered obstacles in his bid for the presidency. Chief among them was the concern that prejudice against Catholics would lose Kennedy too many votes. Some said that a Catholic could never win the presidency. Non-Catholics often worried that, as a Catholic, Kennedy would answer to the pope—and that the pope would, in essence, be running the country.

Others were concerned that JFK was under his father's thumb, since Joe Sr. had financed his son's campaigns and had clearly helped orchestrate his successes. Former President Harry Truman recognized this concern when he said, "It's not the pope I'm afraid of, it's the pop." While some pointed to Kennedy's good looks and charm, others saw it as evidence that he was a "movie star" candidate who had been groomed by his father's money and effective publicity.

Kennedy worked hard to combat these perceptions. At an important campaign stop during the West Virginia primary, he said, "I am a Catholic, but the fact that I was born a Catholic, does that mean that I can't be the president of the U.S.? I'm able to serve in Congress and my brother was able to give his life, but we can't be president?"

★★★★★★★★★★★★★★★★★

## Catholic Candidates

John F. Kennedy was not the first Catholic presidential candidate. Al Smith, governor of New York, was nominated by the Democratic Party in 1928. He lost the election to Herbert Hoover.

In 2004, Senator John Kerry of Massachusetts became the first Catholic since Kennedy to run for president.

Former first lady Eleanor Roosevelt criticized JFK's failure to condemn Senator Joe McCarthy's anti-communist "witch hunts."

Once JFK received the Democratic Party's nomination for the presidency, he made this issue even clearer in a speech before Protestant ministers in Texas. He said, "I am not the Catholic candidate for president. I am the Democratic Party's candidate for president who happens also to be a Catholic. I do not speak for my church on public matters—and the church does not speak for me." By tackling the voters' concern regarding his religion, Kennedy once again convinced many of them that he was courageous and honest.

It was harder to overcome the perception that Joe was running the show behind the scenes. Former first lady Eleanor Roosevelt, for one, spoke out against Senator Kennedy for that very reason—and because she felt that he had not stepped forward to censure Senator Joseph McCarthy years earlier (see sidebar on page 54). Her criticism was a problem for Kennedy, since she was considered one of the most influential Democrats in the nation at the time. Eventually, JFK met with her and won her over. But the charge about his father never completely disappeared.

In 1960, Senator John F. Kennedy turned forty-three years old, and he had served in Congress for thirteen years. Everything he and his family had worked for was within reach. "The time is now," he said.

JFK campaigns for the 1960 Democratic nomination in the first of the presidential primary elections, in New Hampshire.

# CHAPTER 7

# A Family Effort

*[The challenges of the future are a] new frontier
of unknown opportunities and perils—
a frontier of unfulfilled hopes and threats.*

Jack Kennedy's family had thrown itself into each of his
elections, and the presidency, of course, was the greatest
prize of all. In 1960, only sixteen states used the primary
system; the others chose delegates at state political
conventions instead. In the sixteen Democratic primaries,
Jack had a formidable opponent in Senator Hubert H.
Humphrey from Minnesota. Humphrey had spoken out in
favor of civil rights for African Americans as early as 1949,
whereas Kennedy was criticized for being too timid on the
issue. He had other opponents as well, including Texas
senator Lyndon B. Johnson, Missouri senator Stuart
Symington, and ex-presidential candidate Adlai Stevenson.
But in the 1960 presidential race, only Humphrey was
willing to "mix it up" in the primaries.

Kennedy had no trouble winning the primary in New
Hampshire, where he was well known as a fellow New
Englander and ran virtually unopposed. But if he was
going to prove that he had broad appeal throughout the
United States, he would have to beat Humphrey on his
own Midwestern turf—in Wisconsin. Wisconsin was also
predominantly Protestant, so it was an opportunity for

## Hubert Humphrey

Senator Kennedy beat Minnesota senator Hubert H. Humphrey II to become the Democratic presidential candidate in 1960. But Humphrey did not vanish from the political scene after this defeat. He served as vice president under President Lyndon B. Johnson and was the Democratic Party's candidate in the 1968 presidential election. Humphrey lost that election to Richard M. Nixon, whom Kennedy defeated in 1960.

One of Humphrey's finest moments came at the Democratic National Convention in 1948. He gave a speech telling the convention members that the Democratic Party should support the civil rights movement and walk "into the bright sunshine of human rights."

Kennedy to show that his Catholicism was no barrier to his being elected in a largely Protestant country. The Kennedys swooped down on the state, carrying with them a sense of glamor. They had such a strong presence there that Humphrey complained he felt like "an independent merchant competing against a chain store."

The campaigners included Jack's mother, now seventy years old; his twenty-eight-year-old brother Teddy, the baby of the family; and all his sisters (except Rosemary), who continued to hold tea parties for groups of women to introduce and promote the candidate. Joe Sr. wisely decided to remain in the background, fearful of reviving the accusation that he was the power behind the throne. However, he was still his son's campaign financier, and he worked hard behind the scenes. Jack's brother-in-law Stephen Smith, who was married to Jack's sister

Jean, ran the national campaign organization from Washington, D.C. Another brother-in-law, Sargent Shriver, who was married to Jack's sister Eunice, also campaigned.

Jackie worked tirelessly. In one instance, she took over the microphone at a local store and invited people to continue shopping while she told them about her husband.

But Jack's biggest hands-on help was his brother Bobby, the seventh of the nine children. Bobby managed the day-to-day presidential campaign with the same genius for organization that he had brought to his brother's previous campaigns. Bobby was a scrappy, idealistic bulldog, and he had a way of getting support for Jack from party bosses and other members of the Democratic

Three weeks before the presidential election, Jackie joins JFK for a ticker-tape parade in New York.

Bobby Kennedy talks with West Virginia voters. He worked tirelessly for his brother's presidential campaign.

Party. Throughout JFK's political career, especially during his presidency, Bobby was a guiding force and a trusted adviser who made things happen for his older brother.

It is difficult to imagine another large family making such sacrifices to achieve one member's goal. Some of it can be attributed to the loyalty that Joe and Rose instilled in their children at an early age. And some of it, no doubt, resulted from the unusual sense of family destiny that Joe drummed into the children: Joe's son was going to be the first Catholic president, and everyone was going to pull together to make it happen. That, first and foremost, was the family business, and even those who married into the family practiced it.

JFK himself worked hard and with determination. Still plagued by back pain and other health problems, he nevertheless stood on many cold winter days shaking hands and making speeches throughout Wisconsin. When the dust settled after the April 5 primary, he had won more than 56 percent of the vote— a stunning achievement. But he had been more successful in areas of Wisconsin that had a large Catholic population than in mostly Protestant areas. So the question that haunted Kennedy throughout the campaign remained: Could a Catholic really be elected president?

JFK set out to prove his victory was no fluke. He threw himself into the primary in West Virginia, where 96 percent of the voters were non-Catholics. Once again he confronted the religion issue directly. "Nobody asked me if I was a Catholic when I joined the United States Navy," he told voters. "Nobody asked my brother if he was a Catholic or Protestant before he climbed into an American bomber plane to fly his last mission." It was difficult to argue that war heroes did not merit public office in the country for which they had risked their lives.

JFK campaigns in the coal-mining state of West Virginia, where he promises to fight poverty if elected.

## Robert F. "Bobby" Kennedy

Bobby Kennedy was JFK's campaign manager. Later on, he served as **attorney general** in President Kennedy's **cabinet**.

He was elected New York senator in 1964. In that role he tackled poverty and racism, worked hard for minority rights, and called for an end to the Vietnam War.

Bobby ran for the Democratic presidential nomination in 1968 and was a popular candidate, winning several primaries. On June 4, 1968, he won the primary in the important state of California. Shortly past midnight on June 5, he was fatally shot as he left the Ambassador Hotel in Los Angeles after giving his victory speech. He died early the next day, on June 6.

At the funeral mass for Bobby at St. Patrick's Cathedral in New York, his younger brother Ted Kennedy said that Bobby should be remembered "simply as a good and decent man, who saw wrong and tried to right it, saw suffering and tried to heal it, saw war and tried to stop it."

Kennedy crisscrossed the state, shaking thousands of hands and making as many speeches as possible before the May 10 primary. Jackie, who had to leave the campaign after West Virginia because of a difficult pregnancy, won the hearts of many West Virginia voters when she visited an elderly man who wanted to meet her but could not leave his sick wife. And of course, thanks to his father, Kennedy was able to outspend Hubert Humphrey—and not by a little. The end result of all this effort was a landslide for JFK, with nearly 61 percent of the vote. The defeated Humphrey dropped out of the race.

# The Presidential Candidate

John F. Kennedy had proven that he could successfully win Protestant voters, which would stand him in good stead at the Democratic National Convention in July. He went on to win primaries in other states, including Maryland and Oregon. But when he got to the convention, he still had to face some Democrats who were more interested in Lyndon B. Johnson, Stuart Symington, and Adlai Stevenson. Johnson in particular fought hard, raising questions about how Kennedy's campaign had been funded and his health problems, which were, for the most part, not publicly known. Jack and Bobby Kennedy fought back, keeping track of every delegate's vote and battling to keep the tide from turning against JFK. Eventually Symington dropped out of the race, and Stevenson turned out to have more sentimental support than actual delegates. Johnson remained, however, and he made it a close race until the very end.

Kennedy secured the nomination on the first ballot, but not until the alphabetical roll call of states had reached all the way to Wyoming. That state's fifteen votes put him at the top by a margin of two. He had won the nomination by the slimmest of margins, but he had won it nonetheless.

What happened next was unusual even by the standards of politics. Kennedy picked as his running mate

JFK chose Texas senator Lyndon B. Johnson as his vice-presidential running mate.

67

none other than Lyndon Johnson, who had launched ruthless attacks against him and his family. It was a smart move. Johnson, who led the majority party in the Senate, was from Texas. Kennedy valued Johnson's ability to attract Southern voters to the ticket, and he thought that Johnson's Protestant background might make his own Catholicism less of an issue with some voters. In addition, Kennedy knew that Johnson was the kind of politician who campaigned hard.

In his acceptance speech at the convention, Kennedy sounded a note that was to become a major theme of his presidency. Whereas most politicians tried to attract voters by making promises of things they would do for them, JFK felt the nation was looking to be inspired by a higher purpose. A television audience of millions heard him describe the challenges of the future as a "new frontier of unknown opportunities and perils—a frontier of unfulfilled hopes and threats." He told Americans that they must make a choice "between the public interest and the private comfort—between national greatness and national decline." He wanted people to commit to this new kind of frontier, just as the pioneers had committed themselves to building a nation on the geographical frontier. It was an exciting message, full of hope and promise. Young people in particular responded to the idealism of the call.

*JFK felt the nation was looking to be inspired by a higher purpose.*

In the November elections, Kennedy would face the Republican candidate for president, Richard M. Nixon, who was the vice president under Dwight D. Eisenhower. Though Nixon was only four years older than his rival, he emphasized the many more years of experience he had in public life. Nixon was certainly ahead in early polls, but once again JFK had his family on his side, particularly Bobby, who drove everyone to work hard for a win. By the beginning of September, Kennedy and Nixon were running neck and neck in the polls.

## The Decisive Debate

Most observers feel that what happened on September 26, 1960, ultimately decided the course of the election. On that day, Kennedy and Nixon engaged in the first of four televised debates on issues of national importance. It was the first time TV had been used to beam presidential debates into people's living rooms, and seventy million Americans tuned in. While Kennedy knew how to use the relatively new medium to his advantage, Nixon was not so lucky.

The first-ever televised presidential debate, between John F. Kennedy and Richard M. Nixon, was watched by seventy million viewers.

Viewers saw a Kennedy who was vigorous and relaxed, who appeared healthy and was in command of facts and figures. Nixon, by contrast, looked drawn and tired and seemed nervous. His gray suit blended in with the gray background, whereas Kennedy's dark blue suit stood out and made him appear sharp and fresh. It was Kennedy, not Nixon, who seemed experienced and in control. "Nixon had built up, during the campaign, the idea that he was the only one who could stand up to [the Russian leader] Khrushchev, that a man of maturity was needed," Bobby said later. "The first debate indicated that not only could John Kennedy stand up to Nixon, he could better him, and so it destroyed the whole basis of Mr. Nixon's campaign in one night."

Nevertheless, the November 8 vote was still too close to call. The Kennedys gathered in Bobby's home in Hyannis Port, craning their necks to see the results as they were reported on TV. The Eastern states reported first, and the news was good. But the reports from the Midwest and West made a victory less certain. By the time all the votes were counted, it was the middle of the night, and John F. Kennedy had closed his eyes for a few hours' rest. In the morning, his three-year-old daughter, Caroline, awakened him with the words, "Good morning, Mr. President." A new era had begun.

Three weeks after winning the presidency, JFK follows his daughter, Caroline, out of church.

# CHAPTER 8

# A New Sense of Hope

*Let every nation know…that we shall pay any price, bear any burden, meet any hardship, support any friend, oppose any foe to assure the survival and success of liberty.*

The day dawned crisp and very cold in Washington on January 20, 1961. A raging snowstorm had finished blanketing the capital in white only the night before. A huge crowd gathered near the Capitol steps to hear John F. Kennedy sworn in as the thirty-fifth president of the United States.

John Fitzgerald Kennedy takes the oath of office and becomes the thirty-fifth president of the United States. He is the youngest man—and the first Roman Catholic—ever elected president.

Most people in the crowd were covered head to foot in warm clothing. But not JFK. He stood without a hat or coat, taking the oath of office and delivering one of the most memorable **inaugural addresses** in American history. He spoke about the issues that were on so many Americans' minds: peace, national security, and creating a just and free world. As he had done after receiving the Democratic nomination for president, he stressed the need for average Americans to be more active in making the world a better place.

*He stood without a hat or coat, taking the oath of office and delivering one of the most memorable inaugural addresses in American history.*

"My fellow Americans," he said toward the end of the speech, "ask not what your country can do for you—ask what you can do for your country.

"My fellow citizens of the world, ask not what America will do for you, but what together we can do for the freedom of man."

To the expectant crowd and the waiting nation, the address sounded an inspiring note. Under President Dwight D. Eisenhower, the 1950s had been a calm and settled time in most respects for America. But there was increasing concern among average citizens about the Soviet threat and the potential of nuclear weapons to destroy nations. Cuba, just ninety miles off the coast of the United States, had become a communist regime under Fidel Castro. The civil rights movement at home was promising much conflict and change. There was a sense that the nation and the world were hovering on the brink of a disaster, and many people were looking for a true leader to point the way. On that day in Washington, such a leader seemed poised to take over the reins.

## Part of JFK's Inaugural Address

Let the word go forth from this time and place, to friend and foe alike, that the torch has been passed to a new generation of Americans— born in this century, tempered by war, disciplined by a hard and bitter

A portrait photograph of President John F. Kennedy distributed by the White House.

peace, proud of our ancient heritage, and unwilling to witness or permit the slow undoing of those human rights to which this nation has always been committed, and to which we are committed today at home and around the world.

Let every nation know, whether it wishes us well or ill, that we shall pay any price, bear any burden, meet any hardship, support any friend, oppose any foe to assure the survival and the success of liberty.

. . . So let us begin anew—remembering on both sides that civility is not a sign of weakness, and sincerity is always subject to proof. Let us never negotiate out of fear. But let us never fear to negotiate.

Let both sides explore what problems unite us instead of belaboring those problems which divide us.

. . . In your hands, my fellow citizens, more than mine, will rest the final success or failure of our course.

Many of the ingredients of the Kennedy White House were hinted at by the inauguration itself:

President Kennedy greets Peace Corps volunteers on the White House South Lawn. He told the young volunteers life in the corps would not be easy but it would be rich and satisfying.

- The presence on the podium of nationally celebrated poet Robert Frost showed that this was going to be an administration that encouraged the arts and intellectual pursuits. Frost had written a poem for the occasion, but couldn't read it because the sun was in his eyes. Instead, he recited another of his poems, "The Gift Outright," from memory.

- To sing the national anthem, JFK chose Marian Anderson, an African American who had overcome great prejudice to become one of the country's leading opera and concert singers. This sent a message that people of all races would be included in President Kennedy's New Frontier.

- JFK's refusal to bundle up against the cold symbolized the youth, energy, and vigor (or "vig-ah," as he called it in his Boston accent) that he was bringing in dealing with the nation's problems.

- His wife, Jackie, who was to take an active role in restoring the White House and setting a cultural tone, was there despite the difficult birth of their second child, John Fitzgerald Kennedy Jr., two months earlier.

Marian Anderson

- President Kennedy was surrounded by many of the men who had advised and supported him through his political career and would continue to do so in the White House, including his brother Bobby.

- Most important, his emphasis on the need for ordinary Americans to give rather than to receive would find its expression in such programs as the Peace Corps, which sent idealistic young Americans around the globe to help those in need.

The inauguration was on a Friday. The new president was so eager to get started running the country that he ignored the fact that the next day was a Saturday. He started work by 9 a.m. the following morning and insisted that his aides did, too.

Presidential elections take place in November, but the new president does not take office until January. Between the time of his election in November and his early days as president, JFK worked hard to find the best and brightest men to name to his cabinet. (Unfortunately, he never considered women.) Many of those he chose had been very successful in their own areas of influence: business, academics, politics, and law.

One of the men he selected was Ford Motor Company president Robert S. McNamara, who was to play a huge role in the administration as **secretary of defense**. McNamara was a Harvard graduate who had distinguished himself during World War II as

JFK meets with his secretary of defense, Robert McNamara, in the White House Cabinet Room.

The famous Spanish cellist Pablo Casals was one of the artists who performed at the Kennedy White House.

an air force officer using statistics to make air strikes more effective. He was considered extremely intelligent and able, although some also found him to be arrogant. McNamara was secretary of defense during some of the most intense military crises of the twentieth century, both in Kennedy's administration and that of his successor, Lyndon Johnson.

There were other ways in which President Kennedy helped raise Americans' spirits. Under his administration, the White House became a center for all that was best in American culture—especially art, music, architecture, and ballet. Celebrated musicians such as Pablo Casals, Isaac Stern, and Russian composer Igor Stravinsky performed at the president and first lady's invitation. Ballet, theater, and opera companies gave "command" performances. Famous scientists, scholars, and athletes were invited to dinner. It was a bustling atmosphere, crackling with energy, excellence, and ideas. The youthful, glamorous Kennedys had set Washington on fire after the stodgy years of the Eisenhower administration.

## A White House Restored to Glory

With an article in the September 1961 issue of Life, First Lady Jacqueline Kennedy launched an ambitious project to restore the grandeur of the White House and give it the historic feel that she felt it deserved. Few of the furnishings and paintings reflected a period of history prior to 1948, and she wanted to bring back some furnishings from earlier in the mansion's 161-year history. "The White House belongs to the American people," she said, and set about making it a living museum for them. In dusty, forgotten basement corners, she found dozens of items that had belonged to such historic administrations as Thomas Jefferson's and James Monroe's. When she couldn't find a piece of furniture or a painting from an earlier administration, she coaxed collectors to donate items from that period. In the end, she presented to the American public—in a TV tour watched by millions of people—a White House worthy of the name "America's home."

Jackie Kennedy was determined to make the White House "the first home in the land." She restored each room with great attention to detail.

The president claps as his children, Caroline and John Jr., dance on the Oval Office carpet.

## At Home in the White House

It was the day-to-day life of the young family that most captured the public's imagination and heart. It was clear to all that JFK adored his children and welcomed them to his private office, called the Oval Office, whenever possible. The president's son, John, would hide under his father's desk and spring out to surprise him. One time John insisted on staying for a meeting, and when his father asked his advisers, "What have we got today?" John replied, "I've got a glass of water!"

On another occasion, during an important international crisis, President Kennedy noticed that Caroline had been eating candy just before dinner. "Caroline, have you been eating candy?" he asked. She did not answer, and he repeated the question. Once again she ignored him. Finally, as presidential aide Ted Sorensen relates, "summoning up his full dignity as commander in chief, he asked his daughter, 'Caroline, answer me. Have you been eating candy—yes, no, or maybe?'" Another time, Caroline tottered into her father's press briefing wearing her mother's heels.

The White House was a magical and protected world for the children. There was a playground on the White House lawn and many pets, especially dogs. Americans never tired of hearing about and seeing pictures of the children with their pets, particularly Caroline's pony, Macaroni.

Since the White House contained the president's living quarters as well as his office, JFK was often able to slip away to have lunch with his family. He read to the children at bedtime

Caroline Kennedy rides her famous pony, Macaroni, while the president walks alongside.

and told Caroline fantastic made-up stories about whales. He even quoted poetry to her, which she learned so well that she could correct him if he made a mistake. To please her, President Kennedy would sometimes slip into one of his speeches a line of poetry that they had shared. When Caroline reached the age to start kindergarten, her mother hired a teacher and began a little school in the White House for Caroline and some of her friends. The lessons included reading, phonics, handwriting, story time, French, and music. When Caroline reached the first grade, arithmetic and art were added to the mix.

In all the days of the Kennedy White House, even in the darkest times, Jackie and the children were a bright spot that kept JFK going. As Ted Sorensen later wrote: "No friend ever drew as close to John Kennedy, or contributed so much to his spirit and strength, as his wife, his daughter and his son. He would rather eat fettucine with them in the family dining room than preside over the most important formal banquet in the State Dining Room." After many years of striving, John F. Kennedy was finally home.

The president receives a warm welcome from his children. He loved spending time with them.

# CHAPTER 9

# A Cold War Heats Up

*There are many people in the world who really don't understand...what is the great issue between the free world and the communist world.*

O ne of the terrible burdens of the presidency is having to make life-or-death decisions that affect thousands, or even millions, of people. President Kennedy handled at least two crises when he had just such a decision to make—and both involved Cuba.

When Kennedy took office, Americans were extremely concerned about the presence of a communist regime less than one hundred miles off the coast of Florida. They feared that Cuban president Fidel Castro's partnership with the Soviet Union would lead to more communist governments throughout the hemisphere, particularly in Latin America. The idea of hostile nations on America's doorstep was downright alarming, particularly since the invention of nuclear weapons had made it possible to kill millions of people within distance of missile strikes.

Just days before becoming president, Kennedy was told that

Soviet leader Nikita Khrushchev (right) and Cuba's Fidel Castro meet in Moscow. Their alliance brought the world to the brink of war.

Demonstrators outside the White House oppose the invasion of Cuba, which they fear will bring nuclear war.

the **Central Intelligence Agency (CIA)** had already put in place a secret operation to overthrow Castro. With the authorization of President Eisenhower, the United States was quietly training more than one thousand Cuban exiles who had fled Castro's regime to land in their homeland and spark a revolution. After Kennedy's inauguration, he had to decide whether to continue with this program.

On the one hand, it was thought that the operation could remove the communist regime from power and possibly halt the spread of communism in the region. On the other hand, how would it look for the president to sponsor an invasion of another country so soon after calling for peaceful cooperation among nations in his inaugural address? The Soviet Union and communist China might well use the United States' apparent aggression in Cuba as an excuse to sponsor even more communist regimes throughout the world.

There was also the question of how successful an invasion would be if the president decided to authorize it. Opinions among his advisers differed on this point. The CIA and the military believed that once the Cuban exiles landed, they would be joined by thousands more Cubans living on the island who were eager to overthrow their dictator. In fact, the CIA was so eager to topple Castro that it even recommended sending American forces in as part of the invasion.

The State Department, on the other hand, thought that any invasion—with or without American troops—was a bad idea. Those officials argued that the entire world would assume the United States was behind it, even if all the fighters were Cuban. They predicted that the result would be massive protests around the world. As special assistant to the president Arthur Schlesinger Jr. put it, "At one stroke, it would dissipate all the extraordinary good will which has been rising toward the administration through the world."

When former secretary of state Dean Acheson was told that the Cuban exile force would number fewer than fifteen hundred, who would have to face Castro's twenty-five thousand troops, he

## The Problem with Castro

Fidel Castro became Cuba's leader in the 1959 revolution that overthrew the American-backed government of Fulgencio Batista. Castro immediately promised free democratic elections, but they never took place.

His Communist government confiscated American-owned property and businesses and developed close ties with the Soviet Union. Cuba's relations with the United States have remained shaky under Castro. In January 2005, U.S. Secretary of State Condoleezza Rice called Castro's Cuba one of the world's last remaining "outposts of tyranny."

Castro is one of the world's most durable and recognizable politicians. Cuba's bearded leader has appeared in countless photographs wearing his familiar jungle fatigues and hat. For decades he was rarely seen without one of the island's famous cigars in his mouth or in his hand, but he gave up smoking in the 1980s.

JFK had to make important and difficult decisions about Cuba. He made this doodle about decisions during a cabinet meeting.

said, "It doesn't take Price-Waterhouse [an accounting firm] to figure out that fifteen hundred aren't as good as twenty-five thousand."

Debates about what to do raged within the Kennedy administration for weeks. In the end, JFK followed the advice of the **Joint Chiefs of Staff** and the CIA and authorized the invasion. However, he informed the Cuban exiles that they would be conducting the invasion without direct help from the United States. He wanted to make sure that they understood the risks they were undertaking. Because they wanted to help their own people, they decided to go ahead without any American troops or air support.

## The Bay of Pigs

On April 17, 1961, the invaders landed on the southern coast of Cuba at two beaches on the Bay of Pigs and began fighting. But the hoped-for uprising by Cuban citizens did not happen. By the following evening, most of the invaders had been killed or captured. It was the first major foreign affairs incident of the four-month-old Kennedy administration, and it had been a fiasco.

JFK quickly took responsibility for the defeat. "There is an old saying that victory has a hundred fathers and defeat is an orphan. . . . I am the responsible officer of the government," he said. On a personal level, he was devastated. Jackie told Rose that she had never seen him so low, except after one of his unsuccessful back operations. He had trouble sleeping because he was thinking of the men who had been captured and put into prison in Cuba. During meetings, he would sometimes exclaim, "How could I have been so stupid?"

*"How could I have been so stupid?"*

History has been a little kinder to President Kennedy than he was to himself. He was, as one observer put it, "so new to the presidency that he did not yet know the quality of the men who were offering him advice." The situation required a quick decision, and he made the wrong one. But John F. Kennedy was the kind of president who learned from his mistakes. Privately, he made a note of the lessons to be learned from this episode— which included not relying blindly on military and intelligence advisers.

## The Cuban Missile Crisis

By the time the second crisis involving Cuba began, JFK was a little more settled in the presidency and made some decisions that, according to many, averted a nuclear war. On October 16, 1962, the president's breakfast was interrupted by a visit from his national security adviser, McGeorge Bundy. Bundy had U-2 aircraft reconnaissance photos that proved the Soviet Union was building nuclear missile sites in Cuba. Missiles in the hands of the enemy and so close to the United States would prove a terrible risk.

For the next thirteen days, the president and a small group of advisers met repeatedly to hash out a way to handle the crisis. According to Bobby Kennedy, who was one of the advisers, most of the participants initially wanted to attack the missile sites in Cuba outright, which could have provoked Cuba to launch a nuclear attack on America. As time went on, less drastic ways to proceed were considered. Some wanted to negotiate with the Soviet Union for the voluntary removal of the missiles, perhaps in exchange for a concession from America. For example, America had some missiles on U.S. bases in Turkey, close to the Soviet Union, and the Soviets wanted them removed. One agreement might be that we would remove our missiles if they removed theirs.

An image captured by a U-2 reconnaissance aircraft shows the missile launch site at San Cristobal, Cuba.

A political cartoonist's view of the Cuban Missile Crisis. Khrushchev (left) stores away his missiles while Castro waves a guarantee that the United States will not invade Cuba.

Under the strong recommendation of Secretary of Defense Robert McNamara and others, President Kennedy chose to negotiate, while setting up a naval **blockade** of Cuba. The blockade would prevent Soviet ships from getting through to deliver warheads for the missiles and other weapons. Meanwhile, troops were sent to Florida to prepare for a possible invasion. It was a standoff. Each side was waiting for the other to make the first move.

For nearly two weeks, the world hovered on the brink of a catastrophe. Observers later remarked how calm and focused and rational the president remained throughout the crisis. This time he did not allow his decisions to be rushed. Had he acted like a hothead, who knows what would have happened. Instead, he waited for the Soviet premier Nikita Khrushchev to respond to U.S. demands for the removal of Soviet missiles.

On the evening of October 26, a letter arrived from Khrushchev. It spoke of the dangers of a potential war between the United States and the Soviet Union. It explained that the

Russians were using the missiles to defend Cuba against the United States, since they believed that the U.S. was eager to overthrow Cuba. Khrushchev wrote that if the United States would lift the blockade and pledge not to invade Cuba, the missiles would be removed.

## A Defense Secretary Looks Back

How close did the United States and Cuba come to nuclear war? In 2003, the filmmaker Errol Morris made *The Fog of War: Eleven Lessons from the Life of Robert S. McNamara.* Based in part on a book by former Secretary of Defense Robert McNamara, the documentary film featured McNamara's remembrances about many things, including the Cuban Missile Crisis.

In the film, McNamara revealed that during a panel discussion in Cuba in 1992, some thirty years after the crisis, he had asked Fidel Castro whether he would have recommended the Soviet Union authorize a nuclear attack on the United States if the U.S. had invaded Cuba. Castro responded that he had in fact made such a recommendation, knowing full well that the United States would likely have responded with a missile strike that would have destroyed Cuba. Castro would rather have seen his nation wiped off the face of the earth than watch the United States triumph.

Furthermore, Castro told McNamara that although the CIA believed that the warheads for the missiles had not reached Cuba by the time the blockade began, there were in fact 162 warheads on the island at the height of the crisis. We came within a "hairsbreadth," McNamara said, of a nuclear war that would have resulted in millions of deaths. "At the end," he concluded, "we lucked out."

JFK and Soviet leader Khrushchev meet at the summit conference in the Austrian capital, Vienna, in 1961. The major disagreement at the conference was about Berlin.

Before President Kennedy could respond to this offer, another letter arrived from Russia—this time from others within the Soviet government who took a tougher stance. If the Soviet Union were to remove its missiles from Cuba, they said, the United States must remove the missiles from Turkey.

Kennedy wasn't sure what to do. He wondered who was in charge of the decision making in Moscow, and whether he should respond to the first letter or the second. In the midst of this dilemma, McNamara later recalled, came adviser Llewellyn Thompson, who had once been ambassador to Moscow and had lived with Khrushchev and his wife for a time. Thompson felt that he knew Khrushchev better than anyone in the room, and he argued strongly for a course of negotiation that would allow the Soviet premier to back out gracefully.

What Khrushchev needed in order to back down, Thompson said, was to avoid looking weak to his own people and the Cubans. If Khrushchev withdrew the missiles from Cuba, he had to be able to say afterward that by putting them there in the first place, he had kept the United States from invading Cuba. That way he could end the nuclear showdown without appearing to "give in" to American demands.

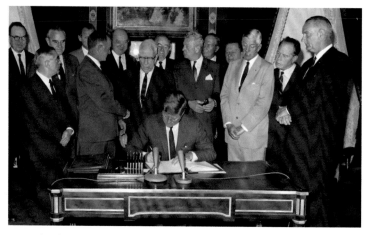

JFK ratifies the treaty banning nuclear weapons tests in the atmosphere, in outer space, and under water. He tells the American people that a limited test ban "is safer by far for the United States than an unlimited nuclear arms race."

With Bobby conducting some of the negotiations, the United States essentially responded to the first proposal: The United States would end the blockade and promise not to invade Cuba in exchange for the removal of the missiles. Privately, Bobby assured the Russian ambassador that once the Soviet missiles were removed from Cuba, the American missiles would be taken out of Turkey. It had been President Kennedy's intention to remove the missiles from Turkey for other reasons all along, but he would not allow the Soviet Union to make the United States look weak.

The whole world breathed a sigh of relief, and President Kennedy proved that he was not only a leader but a great statesman. In 1963, the spirit of cooperation that began with the agreement over Cuba led the United States and the Soviet Union to sign the world's first treaty to control the arms, or weapons, race. The Limited Nuclear Test Ban Treaty banned nuclear tests in space, in the atmosphere, and underwater. It was a beginning. In the decades to follow, there were to be other arms control agreements.

Cuba was not the only place where the Cold War reared its ugly head. At the end of World War II, the Soviet Union occupied the eastern part of Germany. This occupation resulted in the country's being divided into two sections. East Germany became part of what would become known as the Soviet Bloc, which consisted of countries ruled by communist governments closely allied to the Soviet Union. The symbol of a divided Germany—and a divided world—was the Berlin Wall, which separated communist East Berlin from its western half. The citizens of East Berlin were not permitted to leave, not even to visit relatives and friends in West Berlin.

Standing near the Berlin Wall on June 26, 1963, during a visit to Germany, JFK thrilled a crowd of a million cheering West Germans by reinforcing the United States' commitment to freedom for all peoples. "There are many people in the world," he said, "who really don't understand . . . what is the great issue between the free world and the communist world. Let them come to Berlin." In one of his most famous statements, he showed his solidarity with the German people by telling the roaring crowd, *"Ich bin ein Berliner"*— "I am a Berliner." The response was so euphoric that the president later told an aide they would never have another day quite like that one.

The Berlin Wall was erected around West Berlin in August 1961 to stop East Berliners fleeing to the West. JFK visited Berlin in 1963 and gave an inspiring, defiant speech. "All free men," he said, "are citizens of Berlin."

## Personal Loss

Some of the crises JFK faced while in office were extremely personal. In December 1961, Joe Kennedy Sr., who had spent decades of his life steering his son into the presidency, suffered a major stroke. Although he lived for eight more years, he was paralyzed on one side and unable to speak clearly. JFK had lost one of his most trusted advisers and loyal friends, the man most responsible for helping him get to the White House.

Another blow came just before the assassination of the president. In August 1963, Jackie gave birth prematurely to a third child, Patrick Bouvier Kennedy. The baby boy had trouble with his lungs, and he lived only two days. Aide Dave Powers later said, "The loss of Patrick affected the president and Jackie more deeply than anybody, except their closest friends, realized." The president, who had been a fighter all his life, noted that Patrick had "put up quite a fight" to survive. But JFK

The president's father, Joe Sr., suffered a paralyzing stroke in December 1961. He never recovered.

had to put aside his feelings about such personal tragedies and keep the nation's welfare foremost in his mind.

# CHAPTER 10

# A Journey Ended Too Soon

*Please, History, be kind to John F. Kennedy.*
—*Theodore H. White*

About noon on Friday, November 22, 1963, President John F. Kennedy and his wife, Jackie, were seated in the back of an open-topped limousine following a motorcade route through downtown Dallas. Texas governor John Connally and his wife, Nellie, were in the front seat. Some 250,000 people lined the streets, cheering and waving to the first couple, who smiled and waved back. JFK was already thinking about his 1964 reelection campaign, and he knew that Texas voters would be important to his effort. He was pleased the two-day visit to Texas was going so well.

In our current climate of strong security measures to protect against terrorists, it seems incredible that the president should have ridden through such a huge crowd without a bulletproof shield. There was, in fact, a

Escorted by police motor-cyclists, the Kennedys drive through Dallas. Minutes later the president was shot. Texas governor John Connally, who was also wounded by the sniper, sits in the front seat with his wife.

protective bubble top that could have been used that day, but the president wanted the crowds to see him and Jackie clearly. More than once, he had expressed the opinion that if someone wanted to assassinate him, especially a sniper, there wasn't much that could prevent it.

As the motorcade approached Dealey Plaza, and the crowds continued to cheer, Nellie Connally turned to JFK and said, "Mr. President, you certainly cannot say that Dallas doesn't love you."

With that, shots rang out. President Kennedy was hit twice, once in the neck and once in the back of the head. After the first bullet hit, JFK remained upright because of the brace he was wearing for his bad back. If he had slumped forward, he might have escaped the fatal shot that landed in his skull. John Connally was shot in three places—the back, the wrist, and the leg—but he pulled through.

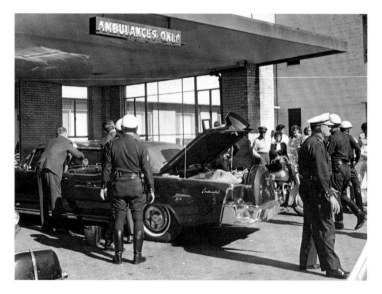

The president's limousine sits outside the hospital emergency room, where doctors try in vain to save his life.

Jackie shouted "Oh, no!" and cradled her husband's head in her lap. At one point, she began to climb back onto the trunk of the car. Secret Service agent Clint Hill swooped down and pushed her back into the limousine, using his body to shield the president from further harm. The car sped off to nearby Parkland Memorial Hospital in a vain attempt to save the president's life.

John Fitzgerald Kennedy, the thirty-fifth president of the United States, was pronounced dead at the hospital at 1 p.m. local time, half an hour after he

Lee Harvey Oswald, President Kennedy's alleged assassin, is led away in handcuffs.

had been shot. The nation and the world went into shock.

Most Americans who were old enough to know what was going on that day remember exactly where they were when they heard the news. It was a terrible blow that plunged the nation into days of mourning. Over the next three days, there was continuous television coverage of the events following the president's death.

Just hours after the assassination, police arrested Lee Harvey Oswald, a loner and communist sympathizer who worked at the Texas School Book Depository, a warehouse that overlooked Dealey Plaza. Oswald had arrived at work earlier that day holding a long, thin package that he later claimed contained curtain rods but could well have hidden a rifle. After the shots were fired, he was seen running from the building. When confronted by police officer J. D. Tippit, Oswald shot and killed Tippit, and then hid out in a movie theater until police found him. A rifle was found in front of a sixth-floor window of the warehouse.

Why did Oswald do it? The world will never know for sure. Two days after JFK's assassination, Americans sat glued to their TVs as Oswald was being transferred from the city jail to the county jail. A man, nightclub owner Jack Ruby, stepped up and assassinated the assassin. As he fired the fatal shot, Ruby is said to have shouted, "You killed my president, you rat!"

The speculation began soon after Oswald's murder. People wondered if Ruby and Oswald were part of some larger plot, and

The Texas School Book Depository on Dealey Plaza, Dallas. Lee Harvey Oswald worked in the building and allegedly shot the president from a sixth-floor window.

Dallas nightclub owner Jack Ruby shoots and fatally wounds Lee Harvey Oswald.

Lyndon B. Johnson takes the presidential oath of office aboard the president's airplane, *Air Force One*. Jackie Kennedy looks on, her clothes still stained by her husband's blood.

if Ruby had killed Oswald to keep him from talking. Who might have wanted the president killed? Fidel Castro? The Soviet Union? Organized crime? Maybe even the CIA? An investigation would have to wait until the nation had buried its president.

After President Kennedy was pronounced dead, his body was flown back to Washington, D.C., on *Air Force One*, the president's plane. Before the plane took off from Texas, Vice President Lyndon Baines Johnson was sworn in as the thirty-sixth president of the United States, with his wife, Lady Bird, on one side, and Jackie Kennedy on the other. She had not yet even changed her bloodstained clothes.

Back in Hyannis Port, the news reached Rose Kennedy. At first she heard that the president was "wounded," and she held out hope that he would pull through. After all, he had survived so many illnesses and operations. Joe had once said, "I know nothing can happen to him. I've stood by his deathbed four times. Each time I said good-bye to him, and he always came back." But this time, Jack did not come back. Bobby called Rose with the terrible news.

Joe, incapacitated by a stroke two years before, may not have fully realized what was going on. "We have told him, but we don't think that he understands it," Rose said. Joe had lost two sons and a daughter, and his dream of having a son in the White House had ended in tragedy. If he didn't quite understand the news, perhaps it was just as well.

## Burial of a President

Jackie decided that the president would be buried in Arlington National Cemetery, a place for heroes, with an eternal flame to mark his grave. McNamara picked the exact spot, which even forty years later brought tears to his eyes as he recalled it to be "the most beautiful spot in Washington." Jackie modeled her husband's funeral arrangements on those for President Abraham Lincoln after his assassination. She was clearly in shock and, in private, sometimes displayed anger. But throughout the ordeal, she remained composed and dignified in public. The entire world marveled at her strength.

*Jackie modeled her husband's funeral arrangements on those for President Abraham Lincoln after his assassination.*

On Sunday, November 24, President John F. Kennedy's body was taken to the Capitol Rotunda by the same horse-drawn carriage that had carried President Franklin Delano Roosevelt's body in 1945. JFK lay in state until the funeral on Monday morning. Some 250,000 mourners filed past the casket—as many as had lined the streets of Dallas, cheering just two days earlier. A nation that had soaked up JFK's inspiring inaugural address on TV now saw a very different scene on their screens.

Men from each of the branches of the armed services carried the president's casket to a carriage for the procession to St. Matthew's Cathedral, where the funeral service was to be held. Behind the carriage was a riderless horse, with boots placed backwards in the stirrups, symbolizing a leader forever lost.

On the day of the funeral, the president's coffin, draped in the stars and stripes, lies outside the Capitol on a gun carriage drawn by six gray horses.

On his third birthday, John Jr. offers his father a farewell salute.

Dignitaries from around the world came to join the funeral procession, including French president Charles de Gaulle, Britain's Prince Philip, West German president Heinrich Lübke, Ethiopian emperor Haile Selassie, and Greece's Queen Frederika.

But it was the gesture of one small boy that captured the world's heart and forever symbolized the nation's heartbreak. As his father's casket was carried from the cathedral, young John Jr., celebrating his third birthday that very day, gave his father a military salute, and the world wept.

## Understanding the Assassination

Not long after, President Johnson authorized a special commission to investigate the assassination and determine whether anyone besides Lee Harvey Oswald had conspired to kill President Kennedy. Named after its head, Chief Justice Earl Warren, the Warren Commission interviewed hundreds of witnesses and experts. On September 24, 1964, it delivered its findings that Oswald, who had once lived in the Soviet Union and had tried unsuccessfully to visit Cuba, had acted alone. This became known as the "lone gunman" theory.

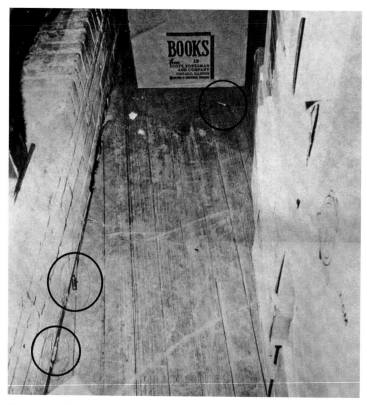

Three used bullet cartridges found on the sixth floor of the Texas School
Book Depository.

According to the commission, Oswald fired three shots from
his sixth-floor perch at the Texas School Book Depository. One
bullet did not find its mark. Another bullet entered the
president's body through his neck, exited, then tore through
Governor Connally, wounding him in three spots. A third bullet
delivered the shattering blow to the president's skull.

In the many years since the assasination, fewer and fewer
Americans have agreed with that conclusion. Some of the
witnesses on that terrible day swore that they heard shots coming

## How They All Fared

The so-called "Kennedy curse" did not end with President Kennedy's death. Bobby Kennedy went into a deep depression after his brother's death. He tried to carry on JFK's work by becoming first a senator from New York and then a candidate for president, as his brother had been before him. But Bobby's life, too, was cut short by an assassin—while he was on the campaign trail, before he could make it to the presidency.

Five years after JFK's death, Jackie married powerful and wealthy Greek businessman Aristotle Onassis. She spent her later years living in New York and working as a book editor. She died of cancer in 1994 and is buried beside John F. Kennedy at Arlington National Cemetery.

Caroline grew up to graduate from law school, write several best-selling books, marry, and have three children—one of whom is named John. Two of her books are *The Best-Loved Poems of Jacqueline Kennedy Onassis* (2001) and *Profiles in Courage for Our Time* (2002), which is a collection of essays that honor modern heroes much as her father had honored the heroes of his time.

Perhaps most tragic of all was the death of John F. Kennedy Jr. The little boy whose last salute to his father forever made him America's son died in 1999 when the plane he was piloting crashed. The crash also took the lives of his wife, Carolyn Bessette Kennedy, and his wife's sister, Lauren Bessette. Though he never entered politics, many had quietly hoped that the thirty-eight-year-old would one day prove heir to his father's Camelot legacy. As with his father, his journey ended too soon.

Jackie marries Aristotle Onassis in 1968.

from a grassy knoll, or hill, near where the president's motorcade passed. *JFK*, a 1991 film by Oliver Stone, raised some disturbing questions about whether Oswald's shots could have done so much damage to the president and Governor Connally. Conspiracy theories have raged for decades, but nothing has ever been proven conclusively.

More than forty years have passed since the tragic murder that robbed the nation and the world of a promising leader. Some have said that an entire generation of Americans, raised on JFK's politics of hope, lost its innocence that day. And some have traced the later protests and unrest of the 1960s "flower children" back to the moment when that innocence was lost.

Even today, Americans consistently rate John F. Kennedy as one of the best presidents of all time.

# CHAPTER 11

# The Legacy of a Better World

*I believe that this nation should commit itself to achieving the goal, before this decade is out, of landing a man on the moon.*

The promise of President Kennedy's all-too-short administration did not end when he died. Many of the ideas he had begun to put into practice were carried out by his successors. Had he lived, JFK would no doubt have taken great pleasure in seeing how the programs he had inspired bore fruit.

Two of those were particularly dear to the president's heart and came to symbolize his optimism and faith in the future. One was the space program, and the other was the Peace Corps.

In 1957, three years before John F. Kennedy was elected president, the Soviet Union had put the first satellite, called *Sputnik*, into space. In the Cold War climate, this sent the United States reeling. Many wondered if Americans were behind the Soviets

The Soviet Union's launch of the tiny *Sputnik* satellite started the space race in 1957.

scientifically, and if science and math instruction in U.S. schools prepared children adequately to explore the new space frontier. In April 1961, the Soviets moved further ahead by launching an astronaut, or cosmonaut, into space. The United States wanted to catch up to the Soviets in what came to be known as the "space race."

But America was not as far behind as many had feared. Less than a month later, on May 5, 1961, astronaut Alan Shepard, a former navy test pilot, became the first American in space. His *Freedom 7* capsule flew for only fifteen minutes but gave Americans hope of great things to come. That same month, President Kennedy sounded the call that inspired more than a decade of intense space exploration: "I believe that this nation

The Kennedys and Vice President Lyndon B. Johnson watch astronaut Alan Shepard become the first American in space.

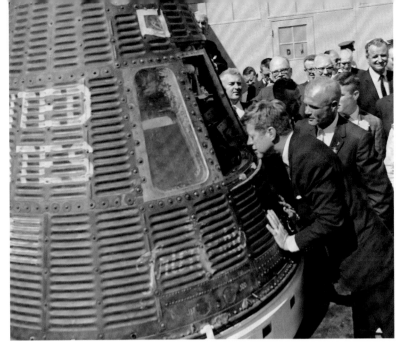

JFK and astronaut John Glenn inspect the spacecraft *Friendship 7*, in which Glenn became the first American to orbit the Earth.

should commit itself to achieving the goal, before this decade is out, of landing a man on the moon and returning him safely to the earth," he told Congress. "No single space project in this period will be more impressive to mankind, or more important for the long-range exploration of space; and none will be so difficult or expensive to accomplish." Kennedy asked Congress to provide enough money to develop the technology to make space exploration happen, and Congress did.

In February 1962, astronaut John Glenn became the first American to orbit the entire Earth in a space capsule. It was the first step toward achieving President Kennedy's dream, and indeed the United States landed a man on the moon by the end of the 1960s. On July 20, 1969, astronauts Neil Armstrong and Edwin "Buzz" Aldrin walked on the moon as the whole world

## The First Men on the Moon

Two of the three *Apollo 11* astronauts walked for two and a half hours on the surface of the moon—and they jumped much higher than they could have on Earth, where gravity is six times more powerful. They carried out scientific experiments and gathered samples of moon rock to bring back to Earth. For protection against the hostile lunar environment, they wore space suits that supplied them with oxygen and also kept the pressure and temperature at safe levels.

How did they return home? The lunar module, *Eagle,* which had landed the astronauts on the moon, became the launch base for an ascent module. This module carried them up to the command module, *Columbia,* in which crew member Michael Collins was orbiting the moon. Once the crew was inside, *Columbia* headed for Earth and re-entered our planet's atmosphere. As it hurtled toward the Earth's surface, parachutes opened and the module landed safely in the Pacific Ocean, where a helicopter picked up the returning heroes.

watched on TV. Many held their breath as Armstrong cautiously put one foot on the lunar surface and said, "That's one small step for man, one giant leap for mankind." It was a bittersweet victory for those who remembered JFK as the man who had inspired America to take the first steps in the direction of space exploration.

## Kennedy's Peace Corps

The Peace Corps was a different kind of project—a chance for Americans to improve life on Earth. In his inaugural address, President Kennedy had challenged citizens to ask not what their country could do for them, but what they could do for their country. Only six weeks after he took office, he gave them the opportunity to respond to that challenge in a concrete way. By executive order, he created the Peace Corps, an organization of American volunteers who would go to different places in the world and help people in underdeveloped countries to build better lives. He put his sister Eunice's husband, Sargent Shriver, in charge of the program, and it thrived.

Thanks to President Kennedy, thousands of Americans have traveled to far-flung places throughout the globe to promote peace and understanding by teaching; providing medical care; improving the local agriculture; or helping to build homes, bridges, and roads.

President Kennedy signs the executive order creating the Peace Corps.

Responding to their president's call, the first Peace Corps volunteers land in Ghana, Africa.

The Peace Corps had three goals: to help the people of interested countries in meeting their need for trained men and women, to help promote a better understanding of Americans among the peoples served, and to help Americans better understand the different peoples of the world. People in struggling countries could see firsthand that, although America was a rich country, some of its citizens cared enough about others to devote two years of their lives to helping those in need. Young people who flocked to the Peace Corps learned much about the richness and value of cultures in Africa, Asia, Latin America, and elsewhere.

*"He set a goal that we could land a man on the moon. Something as far-fetched as that. He didn't live to see it, but we did it."*

Years later, veteran White House reporter Helen Thomas,

who had covered the White House during every presidency from John F. Kennedy to George W. Bush, described John F. Kennedy as the "most inspired" of all those she had covered: "I loved the fact that he told young people to go into public service. He inspired them. He told them they should give something back to the country. He told them that there's a universe out there that we have to explore. He set a goal that we could land a man on the moon. Something as far-fetched as that. He didn't live to see it, but we did it."

## The Vietnam War

President Kennedy tried to be fair and practical in his official dealings with other countries. Just as he had inherited the Bay of Pigs operation from his predecessor, he inherited a military action in Southeast Asia. Less than a decade earlier, Vietnam,

More than 50,000 American troops died in the Vietnam War, which ended in 1975.

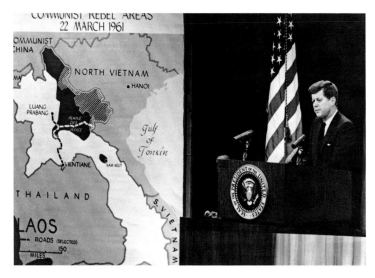

COMMUNIST REBEL AREAS
22 MARCH 1961

COMMUNIST CHINA

NORTH VIETNAM
• HANOI

LUANG PRABANG

PLAINE DES JARRES

Gulf of Tonkin

VIENTIANE    NAM KEUT

THAILAND

S. VIETNAM

LAOS

ROADS (SELECTED)
150
MILES

President Kennedy holds a press conference on Vietnam and Southeast Asia.

Cambodia, and Laos had been French colonies, but communist revolutionaries pushed the French out. When the French left Vietnam in 1954, an international conference divided the country into two parts. North Vietnam, which was communist, was engaged in a war with South Vietnam. Americans saw a danger in the spread of communism and wanted to help South Vietnam fight against it.

During Eisenhower's administration, the U.S. had been supporting the South Vietnamese with money, weapons, and military advisers. JFK continued this assistance, but he did not escalate the situation. The conflict, he said, belonged to the Vietnamese, and they had to win on their own against communist rule. According to Secretary of Defense Robert McNamara and others, the president was on the brink of beginning to withdraw military advisers from Vietnam when he was assassinated.

It's impossible to say with certainty what would have happened if JFK had lived, but many think that America might have avoided a long and costly war in Vietnam—a war that tore America apart and led to the deaths of tens of thousands of Americans and millions of Vietnamese. Under President Kennedy's successors, Lyndon B. Johnson and Richard M. Nixon, the war escalated for more than a decade, until America finally pulled out completely by the end of 1974. South Vietnam fell to the North in April 1975.

## The Civil Rights Movement

Perhaps the most difficult issue facing America during the Kennedy presidency was not in other nations or in outer space, but right at home. Millions of black Americans were being denied their basic rights, particularly in the South. A civil rights movement, led by Dr. Martin Luther King Jr., was attracting national attention by the time JFK became president. Leaders of the civil rights movement wanted African American children to be educated right alongside white children, instead of in segregated second-rate schools. African Americans were tired of having to sit in the back of buses or use separate water fountains or do any of the many things they were legally required to do that made them seem inferior to white people.

*In 1955, a brave woman named Rosa Parks from Montgomery, Alabama, brought attention to the civil rights movement by refusing to give up her bus seat for a white passenger.*

Some progress had been made before JFK became president in 1961, but there was still much to be done. In 1954, the U.S. Supreme Court had ordered an end to segregated schools in a

JFK with leaders of the 1963 March on Washington, on the day Dr. Martin Luther King, Jr. (second from left) delivered his famous "I Have a Dream" speech at the Lincoln Memorial.

famous case called *Brown v. Board of Education* (specifically, the Topeka, Kansas, Board of Education), but there were many places in the country where schools were still not integrated.

In 1955, a brave woman named Rosa Parks from Montgomery, Alabama, brought attention to the civil rights movement by refusing to give up her bus seat for a white passenger. She was arrested, which led black residents to boycott Montgomery city buses for a year. This act of defiance led to an end to **segregation** on city buses.

President Kennedy believed in equal rights for all Americans, but he had to balance that issue against the need for Southern votes when he would seek reelection in 1964. He didn't want to anger the South, but he wanted to help African Americans achieve the equality they had been denied for two centuries.

He had an opportunity to show his commitment to the cause early on. In May 1961, only months after he took office, civil rights **activists** known as Freedom Riders were riding buses in the South, peacefully defying laws that segregated whites and blacks in buses, terminals, and restrooms. When the bus carrying a group of Freedom Riders in Alabama was firebombed and several of the activists were beaten, the president had his brother Bobby, who was the attorney general, take charge of the situation.

Then an African American named James Meredith, who had served his country in the air force, applied for admission to the

Freedom Riders watch a blazing Greyhound bus that was torched near Anniston, Alabama, by a mob opposed to desegregation on buses.

In a televised address on civil rights, the president says it should be possible "for every American to enjoy the privileges of being American without regard to his race or his color."

all-white University of Mississippi. In 1962 the courts ordered the university to admit him, but Mississippi governor Ross Barnett was determined to keep Meredith from enrolling. After Bobby Kennedy tried in vain to persuade the governor to obey the law, President John Kennedy called the Mississippi National Guard into action and ordered more than twenty thousand federal troops to stand ready. As Meredith entered the university in the company of federal marshals, protestors threatened them with bricks and pipes.

President Kennedy went on television that night to persuade Americans of the rightness of the cause. "In a government of laws and not of men, no man, however prominent or powerful, and no mob, however unruly or boisterous, is entitled to defy a court of law," he said. As he was speaking, riots were breaking out on campus. Two people were killed and some two hundred marshals and soldiers were injured before order was restored. When the dust settled, James Meredith had been enrolled at the University of Mississippi, and an important barrier to racial equality was broken.

In June 1963, only months before he died, President Kennedy delivered another televised speech to the nation. This time he made the case for a larger program to ensure racial equality. "When Americans are sent to Vietnam or West Berlin, we do not ask for whites only," he said. Therefore, all Americans should be free to attend public universities and be treated as equals wherever they go— in restaurants, restrooms, on buses, and anywhere else. Soon after the speech, the president presented a civil rights bill to Congress. If enacted, it would have barred discrimination in public places and allowed the attorney general to take action against schools that refused to desegregate.

> *"When Americans are sent to Vietnam or West Berlin, we do not ask for whites only."*

JFK was not able to get the bill through Congress before he died, but that was not the end of civil rights legislation. Eight months after his death, Congress passed the Civil Rights Act of 1964, and in so doing, it honored JFK's memory. As with so many other things, President Kennedy had lain the groundwork for progress.

Historians love to guess what would have happened if President Kennedy had lived. Many think that he probably would have won a second term in 1964, and with no pressure to get reelected after that (since presidents can serve only two full terms), he might have been bolder in pushing programs like civil rights.

In some ways, such speculation misses the point. John F. Kennedy lived his life and served his term as president in such a way that he inspired his fellow Americans to be better citizens, better people. For years after his death, Americans pursued his programs and policies for creating a safer and more just world. The space program, the Peace Corps, a commitment to civil rights, a love of freedom— these were his legacies.

*John F. Kennedy lived his life and his presidency in such a way that he inspired his fellow Americans to be better citizens, better people.*

JFK's deep impact on history is remarkable for the fact that he served a mere one thousand days as president—less than three years. Like a shooting star, he shone brightly, and burned out. But no one who saw that star could ever forget its brilliance.

# GLOSSARY

**activist**—a person campaigning for or against a social or political policy.

**ambassador**—an official sent to represent his government to another nation.

**attorney general**—the chief legal officer in the United States, appointed by the president.

**blockade**—the use of ships or military force to stop supplies from reaching an enemy port, city, or country.

**cabinet**—the executive branch of government made up of people appointed by the president to head government departments and advise the president.

**Central Intelligence Agency (CIA)**—a U.S. government agency that gathers information about governments and individuals who may be deemed a national security threat.

**civil rights**—the protection of individual liberty under the law.

**Cold War**—the hostile relationship between the West (the United States and its allies) and the Soviet Union that existed from about 1947 to 1991.

**communism**—a system of government in which one party holds power, and property is owned by the government or by all the members of a community.

**Congress**—the nation's law-making body, whose members are elected by popular vote.

**congressional district**—the United States is divided into 435 congressional districts. Each one elects a representative to serve for two years.

**House of Representatives**—one of the two houses of Congress. The number of representatives from each state is determined by population size.

**inaugural address**—a speech given by a president entering office.

**Joint Chiefs of Staff**—the highest-ranking members of the armed services who advise the president and the secretary of defense on military matters.

**primary**—an election at which supporters of a political party choose their candidate for an upcoming election.

**secretary of defense**—the person appointed by the president to run the Department of Defense, formulate defense policy, and carry it out.

**segregation**—the separation of people based on their race.

**Senate**—one of the two houses of Congress. Voters in each state elect two representatives to serve in the U.S. Senate.

**Soviet Union**—a global superpower and rival to the United States after World War II, also called the Union of Soviet Socialist Republics or USSR.

**U.S. Securities and Exchange Commission**—a government agency that protects investors from fraud.

**World War II**—a global conflict that began in 1939 and ended in 1945.

# BIBLIOGRAPHY

Dallek, Robert. *An Unfinished Life: John F. Kennedy 1917–1963.* New York: Little Brown and Company, 2003.

Donovan, Robert J. *PT 109: John F. Kennedy in World War II.* New York: McGraw-Hill, 1961, 2001.

Editors of TIME for Kids and Ritu Upadhyay. *John F. Kennedy: The Making of a Leader.* New York: HarperCollins, 2005.

Kaplan, Howard S. *John F. Kennedy: A Photographic Story of a Life.* New York: DK Publishing Inc., 2004.

Kennedy, John F. "A plea for a raise by Jack Kennedy, Dedicated to my father Mr. J. P. Kennedy," undated note. "Justice," undated essay at Choate. John F. Kennedy Library.

Kennedy, John F. "My Brother Joe," *As We Remember Joe,* undated letter, John F. Kennedy Library.

Kennedy, John F. *Profiles in Courage.* New York: HarperCollins, 1956, 2003.

Kennedy, Joseph P., Sr. Letter to Joseph P. Jr., May 4, 1934. John F. Kennedy Library.

Kennedy, Joseph P., Jr. Letter to John F. Kennedy, August 10, 1944. John F. Kennedy Library.

Kennedy, Robert F. *Thirteen Days: A Memoir of the Cuban Missile Crisis.* New York: W. W. Norton and Company, 1971.

Kennedy, Rose. Undated Letter to Choate, John F. Kennedy Library.

Loviny, Christophe, and Vincent Touze. *JFK: Remembering Jack.* San Francisco: Chronicle Books, 2003.

Maher, J. J. Report of Jack Kennedy in His House, The Choate School, undated, John F. Kennedy Library.

McDonough, Yona Zeldis. *Who Was John F. Kennedy?* New York: Grosset and Dunlap, 2005.

Schlesinger, Arthur M., Jr. *A Thousand Days: John F. Kennedy in the White House.* New York: Houghton Mifflin, 1965, 2002.

Smith, Sally Bedell. *Grace and Power: The Private World of the Kennedy White House.* New York: Random House, 2004.

Sommer, Shelley. *John F. Kennedy: His Life and Legacy.* New York: HarperCollins, 2005.

Sorensen, Theodore C. *Kennedy.* Old Saybrook, CT: William S. Konecky Associates, 1995.

St. John, George. General Estimate (John F. Kennedy's Harvard application), undated, John F. Kennedy Library.

White House Historical Association. "The Kennedy White House. Part One:

Recollections," *White House History*, no. 13, Summer 2003.
White, T. H. *In Search of History*, New York: HarperCollins, 1978.

# IMAGE CREDITS

© CORBIS: 64, 65, 87
© Bettmann/CORBIS: 8, 18, 81, 82, 101, 104, 115
© Stanley Tretick/Sygma/CORBIS: 80
Courtesy *The Dallas Morning News*: 93
Dwight D. Eisenhower Library: 53
Courtesy of the Franklin D. Roosevelt Library Digital Archives: 20
Instructional Resources Corporation: 60, 63
© iStockphoto.com/"Roberta Casaliggi": 50
© iStockphoto.com/"Brian Palmer": 49
John F. Kennedy Library, John F. Kennedy Personal Papers, Box 4A: 36
John F. Kennedy Library, President's Office Files, Box 115: 84
John F. Kennedy Library, Rose Kennedy Papers: 12 (top)
Courtesy of the John F. Kennedy Presidential Library and
Museum: 1, 2, 4, 5, 9, 14, 23, 26, 27, 29, 30, 31, 33, 34, 37, 39, 40, 41, 42, 45,
    47, 48, 54, 57, 59, 70, 71, 73, 74 (top), 75, 76, 77, 78, 79, 86, 89, 90, 91,
    92, 94, 98, 100, 106, 107, 112, 114, 116, 119
Joel W. Benjamin, photographer, courtesy of the John F. Kennedy Presidential
    Library and Museum: 35
Toni Frissell, photographer, courtesy of the John F. Kennedy Presidential Library
    and Museum: 55
Copyright John F. Kennedy Library Foundation: 10, 11, 12 (bottom), 19
Library of Congress: 3, 7, 56, 67
Library of Congress/Carl Van Vechten: 74 (bottom)
The Peace Corps: 109, 110
Bret St. Clair/The Sixth Floor Museum at Dealey Plaza: 96
Bill Winfrey, photographer, Tom Dillard Collection, *The Dallas Morning
    News*/The Sixth Floor Museum at Dealey Plaza: 95
*The Standard-Times*, New Bedford, MA: 22
Wikipedia, The Free Encyclopedia: 69, 97, 102, 105, 111
Cover art: AP Images

# ABOUT THE AUTHOR

**Marie Hodge** is a National Magazine Award–winning writer who has
published six books, including the picture book *Are You Sleepy Yet, Petey?*.
She has served as an editor or executive editor at many magazines
throughout the country and has written numerous magazine articles.

# INDEX

Note: Both Jack and JFK refer to John F. Kennedy.

Activists, 115, 120
Addison's disease, iv, 47, 55
Ambassador, 18, 120
Anderson, Marian, 74
Assassination, iv
  conspiracy speculation, 96–98, 101, 102–104
  funeral after, 99–101
  investigation of, 101–104
  Jack Ruby and, 96–98
  Lee Harvey Oswald and, 3, 95–98, 101–104
  *Life* magazine memorial issue and, 5–9
  motorcade and, 93–94
  shots fired, 94–95
  Texas School Book Depository and, 95–96, 102
  worldwide reaction to, 3–4, 101
Attorney general, 66, 120
Bay of Pigs, iv, 84–85
Berlin Wall, 91
Birth, of John F. Kennedy, iv, 10
Blockade, 87, 88, 90, 120
Bouvier, Jacqueline. *See* Kennedy, Jacqueline
Burial, of JFK, iv, 99–101
Cabinet, 66, 75–76, 120
Camelot, 6–9, 53
Castro, Fidel, 72, 81–82, 83, 87, 88, 98. *See also* Cuba
Catholicism
  near-vice-presidential candidacy and, 56
  presidential campaign and, 58, 59, 62, 64–65, 68, 71
Central Intelligence Agency (CIA), 82, 120
Children, of JFK. *See* Kennedy, Caroline; Kennedy, John F., Jr.; Kennedy, Patrick Bouvier
Civil rights movement, 2, 61, 62, 72, 113–118, 120
Cold War, 48, 81–92, 120. *See also* Soviet Union
  avoiding nuclear war and, 87–91
  Bay of Pigs and, 84–85
  blockade of Cuba and, 87, 88, 90

Cuban invasion and, 81–85
Cuban Missile Crisis and, iv, 85–91
Communism, 48, 120. *See also* Cold War; Cuba
  defined, 120
  Senator McCarthy and, 54, 59, 60
  Soviet Union and, 48, 91
  symbol of, 50
  threat of, 48, 49
  Vietnam War and, 112
Congress, 1, 120
Congressional district, 44, 120
Congressman Kennedy, 44–48
  campaign of, 44–46
  election of, iv, 46
  frustration of, 47
  as youngest congressman, 1
Connally, John, 93, 94, 102, 104
Cuba
  Bay of Pigs, iv, 84–85
  blockade of, 87, 88, 90
  communism and, 72, 81–82, 83
  plan to overthrow, 82–84
Cuban Missile Crisis, iv, 85–91
Death, of JFK. *See* Assassination
Democratic Party, defined, 49
Early years. *See also* Family power and privilege
  asking for allowance raise, 24
  birth of JFK, iv, 10
  books Jack loved, 13
  family photo, 11
  family wealth, 19–23
  Joe Jr. and, 11, 15–18, 23, 25
  prep school, 12, 13–18, 21, 22–23
  rivals and friends, 16–18
  sickly childhood, 11–12, 19–20
  thoughts on inequality, 21
  trouble at school, 13–16, 23
Education, iv
  Harvard, 23–25, 27
  prep school, 12, 13–18, 21, 22–23
Eisenhower, Dwight D., 52, 53, 56, 67, 72, 82, 112
Family power and privilege
  early JFK essay on, 21
  European travels and, 25–27

growth of, 20–23
Harvard admission and, 23–25
strong family ties, 28–29
Father. *See* Kennedy, Joseph "Joe," Sr.
Fitzgerald, John Francis "Honey Fitz," 10, 19, 20, 42, 48
Frost, David, 74
Funeral, of JFK, iv, 99–101
Germany, Soviet occupation, 91
Harvard, 23–25, 27
House of Representatives, 48, 120
Humphrey, Senator Hubert H., 61, 62, 66
Hyannis Port home, 22
"*Ich bin ein Berliner,*" 91
Illnesses and pain
  Addison's disease/back pain, iv, 47, 55
  back pain, 47, 55
  as child, 11–12, 19–20
  coma after surgery, 55
  living with pain, 46–47
  presidential campaign and, 64
  risky surgeries, 55, 56
Inaugural address, 72, 73, 120
Johnson, Lyndon B., 61, 62, 67–68, 76, 98, 101, 106, 113
Joint Chiefs of Staff, 84, 120
Kennedy, Caroline, iv, 5, 70, 78, 79–80, 103
Kennedy, Edward "Ted," 11, 28, 36, 62, 66
Kennedy, Eunice, 11, 12, 27, 28, 63
Kennedy, Jacqueline
  assassination and, 92, 95, 98
  death of, 103
  JFK funeral and, 99
  losing child, 92
  marriage to Aristotle Onassis, 103, 104
  marriage to JFK, iv, 52–55
  memories of JFK, 4–9
  presidential campaign and, 63
  restoring White House to glory, 74, 76, 77
Kennedy, Joe, Jr.
  death of, iv, 38–40
  early years, 10, 11

Discover interesting personalities
in the Sterling Biographies® series:

**Marian Anderson:** *A Voice Uplifted*
**Neil Armstrong:** *One Giant Leap for Mankind*
**Alexander Graham Bell:** *Giving Voice to the World*
**Cleopatra:** *Egypt's Last and Greatest Queen*
**Christopher Columbus:** *The Voyage That Changed the World*
**Jacques Cousteau:** *A Life Under the Sea*
**Davy Crockett:** *Frontier Legend*
**Marie Curie:** *Mother of Modern Physics*
**Frederick Douglass:** *Rising Up from Slavery*
**Amelia Earhart:** *A Life in Flight*
**Thomas Edison:** *The Man Who Lit Up the World*
**Albert Einstein:** *The Miracle Mind*
**Anne Frank:** *Hidden Hope*
**Benjamin Franklin:** *Revolutionary Inventor*
**Matthew Henson:** *The Quest for the North Pole*
**Harry Houdini:** *Death-Defying Showman*
**Thomas Jefferson:** *Architect of Freedom*
**Joan of Arc:** *Heavenly Warrior*
**Helen Keller:** *Courage in Darkness*
**John F. Kennedy:** *Voice of Hope*
**Martin Luther King, Jr.:** *A Dream of Hope*
**Lewis & Clark:** *Blazing a Trail West*
**Abraham Lincoln:** *From Pioneer to President*
**Rosa Parks:** *Courageous Citizen*
**Eleanor Roosevelt:** *A Courageous Spirit*
**Franklin Delano Roosevelt:** *A National Hero*
**Harriet Tubman:** *Leading the Way to Freedom*
**George Washington:** *An American Life*
**The Wright Brothers:** *First in Flight*
**Malcolm X:** *A Revolutionary Voice*